on not knowing

on not knowing

HOW TO LOVE AND OTHER ESSAYS

Emily Ogden

THE UNIVERSITY OF CHICAGO PRESS

The University of Chicago Press, Chicago 60637
Published 2022
Printed in the United States of America

31 30 29 28 27 26 25 24 23 22   1 2 3 4 5

ISBN-13: 978-0-226-75121-4 (cloth)
ISBN-13: 978-0-226-75135-1 (paper)
ISBN-13: 978-0-226-75149-8 (e-book)
DOI: https://doi.org/10.7208/chicago/9780226751498.001.0001

Page v: the epigraphs are from Herman Melville, *Moby-Dick; or, The Whale*
(Evanston, IL: Northwestern University Press, 1988), 134, quoting John
Hunter; and Elizabeth Hardwick, *Sleepless Nights* (New York: New York Review
Books, 2001), 5.

Library of Congress Cataloging-in-Publication Data

Names: Ogden, Emily, author.
Title: On not knowing : how to love and other essays / Emily Ogden.
Description: Chicago : The University of Chicago Press, 2022.
Identifiers: LCCN 2021035770 | ISBN 9780226751214 (cloth) | ISBN
9780226751351 (paperback) | ISBN 9780226751498 (ebook)
Subjects: LCGFT: Essays.
Classification: LCC PS3615.G36 O6 2022 | DDC 814/.6—dc23
LC record available at https://lccn.loc.gov/2021035770

♾ This paper meets the requirements of ANSI/NISO Z39.48-1992
(Permanence of Paper).

Unfitness to pursue our research in the unfathomable waters.

Herman Melville

Looking for the fossilized, for something—persons and places thick and encrusted with final shape; instead there are many, many minnows, wildly swimming, trembling, vigilant to escape the net.

Elizabeth Hardwick

contents

on not knowing

how to catch a minnow

The world burns, yet the fire is not bright enough to read a map by. Nor am I mostly reading. I am still sweeping the dirt out of the corners and intercepting my children's arms halfway through the act of smashing a glass on the stone ground. I am still trying to use fruit before it rots. The light flickers.

Revelation is no common thing. When it comes, it rarely lasts. It is not necessarily present at the end of the world. How to love, what to do, in the dim times? These are the questions of *On Not Knowing*.

From the Book of Revelation in the Bible, most people remember the apocalyptic prophecy. But the book begins with ordinary failures. A sword-mouthed being dictates John the Revelator's letters to the seven churches of Asia Minor, present-day Turkey. The angel scolds Pergamum for worshipping false idols. He tells Sardis, "Wake up."[1] In the letter to Ephesus, he complains: "I have this against you, that you have abandoned the love you had at first."[2]

Before the end of the world, even while the world is ending, the Book of Revelation concerns itself with dailiness, as though there were a close relationship between the lightning strike and the dimness into which it subsides. The world has mundanity, duration, bullshit. Many nonsense tasks must be completed; false spirits must be tried and rejected; long periods pass in which nothing illuminating happens. Write to Sardis and tell them it can never add up. Write to Pergamum and tell them, you still have to hold your children, fetch them tissues, and find boxes for their caterpillars.

Leviathan threatens. Mostly I see minnows.

"Looking for the fossilized, for something—persons and places thick and encrusted with final shape," writes Elizabeth Hardwick; "instead there are many, many minnows, wildly swimming, trembling, vigilant to escape the net."[3] A person can want a clear view and not get it; a person can believe decisive action is required and yet not know how to begin. "I would up heart, were it not like lead. But my whole clock's run down; my heart the all-controlling weight, I have no key to lift again."[4] So says Starbuck, the first mate of the *Pequod*, in *Moby-Dick*, overmatched by the tyranny of Ahab. Unfitness to pursue our research in the unfathomable waters; unfitness to act too. To see the encrusted form might be best, but to attend to the minnows as they present themselves is better than to feign a monumental vision and live by it. In this book, I try to resist the temptation to turn away from things as I find them—blurry, quicksilver, unhandsome.

At the edge of a midsummer river, a handful of minnows hangs in the bright brown light. Their silver noses point toward the branch that shelters them from the current. They hover with the busy motionlessness of bees. Minnows call the hand. Without decision, my arm darts out. The fish sense my intention propagating itself toward them. They have lateral line organs that permit them to feel, as a kind of matrix, the motions of others in the water. They are gone so fast it is as if their leaving caused my fingers to touch the river, and not the other way around.

It is troublesome enough to catch a single minnow in a stream; now imagine a whole school of herring, radiating silver from every point. Massive schools may improve the odds of survival for any individual fish, although it is not clear why. It might be the case that marine predators struggle to focalize upon a single fish among many. It is not that they are bad at focusing, but that they are too good at it. Their targeting capacity is too easily triggered; the impulse to fix every fish in their sights prevents them from sighting a single one completely. They start to fix their eyes on one. Before they have even begun, they get distracted by another one and try to focus on it instead. The process is never complete.[5]

A human being, also a predator, will find it impossible to keep an eye on one starling in a flock of thousands. Conceptual efforts stumble in the face of the world's vast calamitous tides. Nonetheless, it is human beings who, in the aggregate, have set those tides on foot. No act, no failure to act, no use or squandering of resources that does not mark me as the author of another's destruction. Orca-like, I can't focus; minnow-like, I respond unthinkingly to the fact of others' turning. In the execution of my acts, I entail action on others in my turn. As difficult as it is for me to think one thought among a proliferation of thoughts, I would appear to be, at the same time, effortlessly prolific in my complicity. My school has destroyed a planet.

Unknowing is on every side of the predicament. Unknowing is there in the terminal flight into frozen innocence with which some of us try to protect ourselves from knowledge of our culpability. Unknowing is there, too, in the uncertainty one may feel when confronted with the problem of how to repair the damage. And unknowing will still be there if one finds a way to live that one can live with. For the few fish captured, many more will escape the net.

If there is a kind of unknowing that could serve now, it is not the defensiveness of willful ignorance but the defenselessness of not knowing yet. Can a person go back to the unpruned adjectives of immediate experience? Before one summed up this moment in history, what, exactly, was it? What, lying under the summary—what, swimming chaotically beneath any pretense of certainty—what, before the predator's eye confounded itself—what was it, what does it continue to be? When I talk about *unknowing*, I am not talking about the refusal to know what can be known, or about the simple accident of not having found something out yet, nor even, although this is warmer, about the fact that we will each absorb only a finite amount of knowledge in the course of our finite lives. Instead, I am talking about a capacity to hold the position of not knowing yet—possibly of not knowing ever. I'm talking about living with the dimness that I will mostly inhabit.

A person might object, but what is so difficult about that? Surely my daily labors, my uncertainties, and my limitations will all be more than sufficiently forced upon me, without my going in search of them. But I am not sure this is true. It seems to me that instead, the moments of angelic clarity tend to overrepresent themselves in my mind. It seems to me that a person might be tempted to live by these moments too much; one might hold too hard to them, wanting to have scales forever falling from one's eyes and lightning forever striking. It seems to me that counterfeiting final shapes and holding to them is a temptation.

I do not think I am unduly skeptical about moments of

heightened experience. Like most people, I can point to a handful of them in my life. There was the rocketing of an owl; the surfacing of a whale; eye contact with a bluegill or a poet, across a line; good sex; the wish for sex with one particular person; and forced sex too; and the advent of danger, such as a copperhead on the asphalt path, or my three-year-old child slipping, with the small obscene splash of Breughel's Icarus, from the dock into the pond, his father following quicker than my sluggish thought to surface him, coughing, sobbing; the child aware despite our studied nonchalance that something he had not known that he possessed had been at stake: his life.

It is true that our lives can be at stake in moments of breakthrough. These moments often change us, sometimes against our will. Other times they change us *with* our will; perhaps we even will the change too hard. Our problem as we see it is how to get bound securely enough. How, we ask ourselves, can we constrain ourselves so tightly that we will never abandon the love we had at first? How can we wake up, and stay that way?

It can be good to attend to moments of passion, clarity, revelation, ecstasy, discovery. It can be good to listen to warnings. But it is in the nature of these moments to slip away. Lightning flashes are brief. In any attempt to bind these moments, there is a risk. These attempts can leave us living by and bound by something, yes, but not by the surprise that broke over us once; by, instead, an impoverished version of that surprise: less threatening, but also less nourishing. As the psychoanalyst and philosopher Anne Dufourmantelle writes, "this is perhaps the danger of 'eventness'; the temptation would perhaps be to outsource the process, to posit the most perfect horizon possible, to recreate the whole protocol, the conditions of the happening of the event, and thereby, in fact,

essentially to repress it."[6] In my very attempt to be durably
changed by something, to incorporate it into my life in a last-
ing way, to *routinize* it, I abandon the love I had at first. And
worse, I proof myself against the breaking of a new love—or
against the resurgence of the old one. Bathed in klieg lights,
I am underwhelmed by lightning; I do not notice lightning
bugs at all.

In this book, I look for my cure in my blurriest, fleetest
experiences; the ones, like childbirth and the care of small
children, that most constrain me to admit I am living an uni-
lluminated and unmonumental life. I want to look at these
trembling things and not only at the monumentalities solicit-
ing my attention. I want to capture something of the experience of dread, guilt, and an almost erotic lassitude that besets
me. On one side the ghastly spectacles of sin and sovereignty;
on the other the child heroes and the saints; at my feet the
dailiness and the mediocrity and the quicksilver evasiveness of the minnows, swimming straight out from my body
through the middle of things, as I time loads of laundry, manage wounded feelings, check whether it will rain, read some
book. These insignificant little fish are what it falls to me to
describe. There is no special merit in it. But it may be better
to say the things that are indefensible, than to cast around for
a defensible thing to say.

It is not impossible that these minnows will trace the out-
lines of a whale. Schools of herring viewed from above will
appear to split around a troubling object, such as a predator
orca, revealing, by their combined undirected movements,
the shape of the threat. As if, although I never could see the
massive submerged body of the whale, I might see his nega-
tive image in the pressure lines of the herring school splitting

and swimming around him, a chance configuration over in seconds. Ten thousand sprats to apprehend a whale. In the trembling of the minnows, in the busy chaos of our unknowing, the Leviathan that is hunting us and that we are might become visible.

how to swim

Once, in the harbor of the Greek island of Patmos, I swam out very far, past all the other swimmers, to where I seemed to be on a level with the edge where the harbor gave way to the open water. Hanging there in the aquamarine light, I was seized by what I can only describe as a fear of depths. As with the fear of heights, the anxiety came from dislocation in a vast space. It felt to me as if something was poised to porpoise up from the rocks I could make out below. It would float up toward me with a slow, sickening grace. I would watch like paralyzed prey. My heart would bludgeon itself to death. But there are no monsters in the Aegean, not even much in the way of big fish or seals. There was nothing beneath me but depth itself. The vast, clear, open expanses around my body were what I feared. I was dislocated, unrelated, free.

"Where do we find ourselves? In a series of which we do not know the extremes, and believe that it has none," writes Ralph Waldo Emerson, in "Experience."[1] The little pleasure boat of the conscious self is built for harbors, but it finds itself often enough on the open ocean, whose swells authorize it and undermine it, buoy it up at times, and at other times, swamp it. That sea is ourself behind ourself, as Emily Dickinson put it: "Ourself behind ourself, Concealed—/ Should startle most—."[2] The sea is us, but not how we think of ourselves; us, but also the history and the social patterns that we were born into, and out of which those jaunty little entities we call selves were fitted together. What relations should pleasure boats establish with the sea?

I used to go kayaking during the summers on the central coast of California. At that time of year, huge populations of an open-water bird called a sooty shearwater come near the shore. Sooties look like black gulls, only smaller and with narrower wings—therefore sharper in their turns. But a person rarely sees these qualities up close. The birds spend most of their lives on the wing, and when they stop, to nest or sleep, they alight on guano-covered rocks out at sea. Only in August, when sardines and anchovies run, do the birds follow the schools of fish to within a mile of the coast. They form flocks in the tens of thousands, draping themselves along the bay, turning in massive counterclockwise gyres as they hunt. They remain far enough away that only the flock's vast social organization is visible, never an individual bird. I couldn't get a feel for them, in the way I know the robin's eye, beady but strangely affecting, or the nuthatch's pert way of zig-zagging, beak first, down the trunk of an oak tree, while chirping his soft clown whistle.

I wanted to see a sooty's eye. As I watched the birds' vast exercises every summer, I tried without success to time my kayak trips for the mornings when they were near shore. Then one day I got lucky. I had already rented a kayak for the day when I saw the sooties. I dragged the boat to the water's edge and pushed in. Sand ground the plastic hull, then kelp lashed it, then nothing. The water glistened, black as mercury. I turned south, toward the birds.

Pulling toward a flock is like flying into a cloud. The sharp edge I perceived from far away turned out not to exist. Instead there were shreds of the flock fraying all over the bay, flyaways too small to perceive from a distance. Lines of birds formed and poured in one direction. There was a gathering sense of event. News of the same fish that brought the sooties had reached every hunting animal. They all had their noses combed toward the south. With each hundred feet our difference from the ordinary increased; every mammal was activated, intent; no gull was preening. The cormorants flapped laboriously in their low-slung lines; the pelicans drafted along the crests of waves. Seals and dolphins muscled over that way; sea lions did their peculiar butterfly stroke. After a while we must have reached the edge of the school of fish because the sea lions stopped to hunt splashingly all around me, their flippers breaching as they maneuvered. Guano's sharp, sour stink, strangely tonic, reached us as it wafted from twenty thousand wings. But the birds themselves were still far away.

I wanted to get closer and I was just setting off when, with a strange modesty, as if she were no thunderclap at all, a whale surfaced within thirty feet of me. Her black spine just barely rolled out of the black shiny water. She was ahead of me, swimming away. Probably she was a humpback; cows with their calves come into the bay this time of year. I was thrilled to see her. I thought I would come alongside her, and I paddled as quickly as I could through the water, fearing I would be too slow. She surfaced once more. But now I saw I had made a great mistake about the nature of my problem. Not *too far away, too close*. She had turned and closed the distance between us. She was no more than a boat length away—that is to say, the part of her I could see was no more than a boat length away. Her head must have been below my keel, nosing the floor of the world out from underneath me. I tried to set off at a panicked sprint, but it is hard to panic in a kayak; they are slow boats. I doubt my poky rate of progress had anything to do with the fact that we never saw each other again. It must be that she gently dove, without making a wave, without ever realizing I was there.

There is nothing like these eruptions from a lower world to make one feel the flimsiness of one's outermost defenses. How those ill-anchored palisades shudder at the slightest blow! What if she had flicked her tail out of the water as she dove? Of the sperm whale's tail, Herman Melville wrote, "Could annihilation occur to matter, this were the thing to do it."[3]

Leviathan: that which we can never see or grasp, but which is permitted to kill us nonetheless. It may be nature, it may be society, and it may be the Antichrist; as to our unfitness to meet it in hand-to-hand combat, there is little to choose between them. The Leviathan of the Hebrew Bible is a great sea monster, perhaps originally a serpent, later a whale. The dragon of Revelation, who rises out of the sea with ten horns and seven heads, is Leviathan; could Leviathan also be a word for John the Revelator's vision swimming up from beneath him, too much for him, on the verge of staving his boat?[4] The Leviathan of Thomas Hobbes is society: a great beast, all of whose coils are never visible to us, coiling back in time before us and surviving after us.

"The sea is history," Derek Walcott says.[5] "I knew that before I knew it was history I was looking at," Dionne Brand replies. Of a childhood in the village of Guayguayare (also called Guaya), on the island of Trinidad, Brand writes, "The sea would forever be larger than me. My eyes hit only its waist. . . . It always came in a jagged circle, frothing and steaming. It reduced all life to its unimportant random meaning. Only we were changing and struggling, living as if everything was urgent, feeling—the ocean was bigger than feeling. It lay at the back of us, on the borders of quarrels and disagreements."[6] Brand's *A Map to the Door of No Return* charts the history of the Black diaspora as if it were the sea, and the sea as if it were the history of this diaspora. When she describes a geometry book that "had lain in the drawer for years as companion to *The Black Napoleon*," as "pages of drawings, signs and symbols with thick dense writing which I could not follow, though I remember elaborate structures, a kind of inexplicable intelligence which I knew I would never conquer but felt I ought to," she is also describing the experience of being born into a history she can never grasp, but that shapes her nonetheless.[7] The sea is a metaphysical and a historical substrate, given to her (as she was given to it) before she became aware. Already under her.[8]

They mingle with each other, the metaphysical terror and the historical one, the salt and the blood, the sea and the social. One Leviathan is no less dramatically out of scale with our individual capacities than the other. As Émile Durkheim had it, culture, though a human creation, was nonetheless received as nature by us. Our minds were neither the blank slates that John Locke imagined nor were they furnished with the innate ideas whose existence Locke doubted. Instead, the way we perceived the most basic categories, such as space and time, was given to us in infancy by the culture into which we were born. Durkheim called these givens "collective representations."[9] The world we received as given, the one that formed our perceptions fundamentally, was both nature and culture. It was both kinds of Leviathan.

One can call this cultural placenta an "unconscious" of sorts, but in the sense of the term that the anthropologist Edward Sapir uses when he refers to "the unconscious patterning of behavior in society."[10] Sapir's unconscious is not an upsurging beast. It is a structuring matrix, a substance on which we are buoyed up. It is not really possible to make sense of how anyone floats along, or for that matter, how anyone drowns, without presuming the existence of a tremendous amount of social information, including "essentially arbitrary modes of interpretation that social tradition is constantly suggesting to us from the very moment of our birth."[11] Human beings have what Sapir calls "intuition" about all that social information. Intuition is not mystical here; it amounts instead to a tact about how to live, a "very delicately nuanced feeling of subtle relations, both experienced and possible."[12] We often have the experience, Sapir thought, of discovering that what felt like a free action was really motivated by loyalty to a finely perceived but inarticulable form. "There are polite and impolite ways of breathing."[13]

With their injustices and cruelties, and with their mercies and their beauties, too, Leviathans nurse us. Nourishment and predation become entangled like an umbilical cord and a whale line. In *Moby-Dick*, Melville comments of a baby whale's umbilical cord that, "not seldom in the rapid vicissitudes of the chase, this natural line, with the maternal end loose, becomes entangled with the hempen one, so that the cub is thereby trapped."[14] We cut our children's umbilical cords at birth only to entangle them in the hempen lines of their language, their culture.

The placenta connects to the child by the umbilical cord

and attaches, on the other side, to the mother's uterus. The placenta is the only organ that is a genetic chimera. In mythology, the chimera is a monster with parts from multiple animals; in biological terms, it is tissue containing cells with more than one genetic makeup. The placenta contains some cells supplied by the mother and some cells supplied by the growing child. Thus the child partly nourishes itself. Culture and language are like a placenta to us: the growing child contributes cells to them; history, a cursing and a nourishing mother, does too.

how to hold it together

I was pregnant with twins when I cast my ballot in the 2016 presidential election. My sons were born not long after the inauguration, under what I could not help feeling was an ill star—although in themselves they are privileged and want for nothing. Nothing, that is, except a planet whose future is secure and a nation that does not "[reign] without a rival" for "revolting barbarity and shameless hypocrisy"—words of Frederick Douglass's whose restless sound wave has kept propagating itself.[1] My sons could not yet crawl when white supremacists marched in downtown Charlottesville, a mile from our house, in August 2017. They started walking at about the time that NPR played recordings of children wailing in detention centers. Just before they turned three, their preschool closed because of the COVID-19 pandemic, and in the summer of 2020, they went with me to one protest and watched me leave for others.

No crisis that has come has passed. My children, mostly but no longer completely oblivious to the world beyond their walls, are asking for stories. "Story bout that," they say when some event, or more commonly some non-event, captures their attention. In the dark, Beckettian world of their fictions, little happens except for a persistent breaching of bodily integrity. Here are the stories; judge for yourself (L. and N. are my sons, and Zeke is one of our dogs):

When L. got stung by a bee
When N. got stung by an ant
When N. got a splinter in his foot
When a wheel fell off the neighbor's pickup truck
When Zeke broke the snake
When Zeke broke the lizard
When the weather broke
When a bowl broke
When L. had broken skin
When the red balloon went up to the ceiling and we
    couldn't reach
When Zeke got out the front door
When N. was coughing so hard he gagged
When the red baby cried

Things break and people break and we, the tellers of stories, survive. That is the common burden of these monotonous, unstructured downers, each of which I have been ordered to tell at least fifty times. My sons listen, calm as sucklings. Why such an appetite for damage? It reflects their reality, I suppose. Toddlers fall and they destroy things. I understand the appeal of Humpty Dumpty without the need to search for royalist intimations. An egg, who is at once a fragile person and a fragile object, shatters beyond repair. Welcome to my household. My sons have had several great falls each, and they have broken literally dozens of literal eggs.

It is pleasant to think about the drama of shattered glass

and consoling to remember that when you split your lip, you get a popsicle. But there is a lower layer, having to do with how we find out what the right edges are to ourselves and other people. It seems to me my sons have had to figure out empirically which are the inalienable parts of their bodies. They asked me to take their ears off for them once. They had tried to remove them but couldn't. It did not necessarily follow that the ears were permanently attached; daily experience proves that many things physically impossible to them are possible to me—unscrewing jars, taking their shirts off. "Cats have paws," N. explained to me when he was nearly two. "Can't take them off." I was startled, at first, to hear the tacit made explicit. Then I remembered that I used to have a recurring nightmare. I grew up with a declawed cat, and I used to dream that my family had amputated his feet.

Sigmund Freud's theories around castration anxiety no longer seem far-fetched to me; in fact, they seem if anything too narrowly applied. One of Freud's ideas on this subject, from the 1927 essay "Fetishism," is that a boy interprets his mother's lack of a penis as the result of castration.[2] Then the boy worries that he will be subject to the same fate. It is hard to know whether the story Freud tells is precisely the right one. But as to the idea that penises may be removable: yes. At my house, we are preoccupied. We have thoroughly ventilated the questions of whether penises are attached and of who does and does not have one. And it's not only penises. It's anything that protrudes from the body as though threatening to become an independent object. The boundaries of bodies, one's own and other people's, have to be discovered in the most fundamental ways—to a degree you can hardly believe—and there is no reason to exclude the possibility that this process is traumatic. What is it like, when you know cats'

paws don't come off without cruel violence, to remember
that you once conceived the plan to remove them? How do
you feel about the crime you contemplated, before you knew
it was a crime?

As to what, then, my sons are using stories for—as to why
stories of breakage rivet them so completely—I think that riv-
eting is more than the affective result. It is also the theme,
the purpose, the cognitive work. They are using their stories
of breakage precisely to rivet things together. Each break is a
testament to one particular wholeness and not another. What
disintegrates acquires, after the fact, an aura of former inte-
gration. It matters, too, that we the tellers are still speaking.
If we are speaking, then we must have withstood the shattering force. In this world where everything that is stitched
together got that way by strong conceptual effort, and where,
at the same time, things seem so very ready to explode again,
it is good to know that the thread of speech floats over all the
calamity.

Stories suture up our parts against a primordial awareness
that we are in pieces. They knit our bodies and our worlds
into shapes we can use and that make sense to us, shapes that
can break and be repaired in sufficiently predictable ways
to allow us to live. I do not mean that there was an original
wholeness; the opposite, in fact. Stories make these shapes
out of a prior, if not original, perception of fragments. They
precede the birth of any one of us, accompanying any possible language or nourishment we could acquire.

"Story bout that," my sons say. "Story BOUT THAT,"
they say more loudly. If still nothing, they poke their fingers
into my mouth, as if to say, take the stories out of there and
give them to us. Detach them from your body and attach
them to ours. They want "stories from the mouth," as ethnog-

rapher Pamela Klassen calls the stories we tell as opposed to the ones we write down.[3] Would it threaten life and limb if I refused? Yes, in a way, it would. I know that the lack of stories would not kill them. They do not yet know what killing is. They are still knitting life and limb together into a wholeness they can recognize as theirs to preserve. They need stories about that.

how to give birth

Language . . . is linked, by breath, to the fact of arriving in life because an other carried you, named you, prattled to you, hoped for you, dreaded you, sung to you, and delivered you—what is called *being born*.

Anne Dufourmantelle, *In Praise of Risk*

When children acquire a natal tongue, an other also gives it. Language, like life, is gestated. One person's language is temporarily grafted onto another's until autonomous speech is possible. The child points and exclaims, and the caretaker supplies a word; the caretaker supplies the stories that the child's hunger demands. You can't help it. Children throw themselves at the world. They have the same sick appetite for pattern as any mammal; they are as ready to expend truly sacrificial levels of energy as any puppy. But because they are human, the spitting kinetic fireball of their life goes into language. They speak—constantly, at length—and you have to answer.

In this process of translation, the mother tongue—like the mother's body—gets bent and stretched, and turns strange.

Carrying my sons cocked out my hips, unzipped my rectus abdominus muscles, changed my mind. Carrying their language also altered mine. A gap opened up in it, an imperceptible sickening at first; then, as with the rush of relaxin, the hormone that opens all your joints so that your hips can stretch, the joints of phoneme, word, and meaning came a little bit undone, to make room. They disarticulated. "I asked my friend the translator, What was the first known act of translation in the history of mankind?" writes Mary Ruefle. "His answer was, Probably something into or out of Egyptian. I thought about this for a while and ventured a certainty: No, I said, it was when a mother heard her baby babble or cry, and had to decide in an instant what it meant."[1]

Language stopped working in its usual ways around the time of quickening; that is to say, long before my sons were born. *The quickening* is an old name for the start of life, marked from the moment when the mother first feels the fetus stir.[2] What I felt was what it must be like for the shallows of the river, when a minnow suddenly darts across. In my belly there was a displacement of water, the swift sharp pulse of a moving fish. When did it start, though? By the time I noticed it, *notice* was not an adequate word. When I *noticed* was only when I gathered up the inklings of an earlier beginning I had not yet claimed as one. By the time I was sure it was the babies, not my intestines, not a flutter of my cramping muscles, I realized I had known it was the babies for a long time.

Should I call them *babies*? Should I call it *life*? The problem is much the same as it is with marking the first movement or the first word: I call them babies, I call it life because they *will have been* babies and it *will have been* life, when they are born. There is no marking of beginnings without a marking of middles and ends. Babbling, too, can only cross over into language because, eventually, it will have already crossed over into language. When is it a word the child is speaking, standing in the crib, disoriented, discontented, saying *ma ma ma ma ma ma*? When is he calling a name and not filling the distance between himself and my coming with the sound of his lips battering themselves against each other? Can I claim it is me he means and no other? One day I can, and then I think it never was not me. And I am both right and wrong: it was me to the extent that pronouns existed at all, which is to say, to the extent that there was separation between persons. But there was not always.

Before the infant learns to be a separate person, there is at first an undifferentiated sea, herself and her mother, a sea that stretches thin when her mother is gone—painfully attenuates—and then rebounds. When otter mothers dive down to fish for crabs and urchins clinging to the rocks, they first tie up their babies in the kelp. Kelp plants are like underwater trees; they root to a rock and then rise up in stiff, buoyant tubes toward the surface of the water, where their fronds make the treetops that otters fish in and kayaks whisper over. The whole time the babies are at anchor, they squeak regularly, so their mothers can return. *Mama* at first is like the otter pup's cry to his diving mother: a homing beacon to bridge this distance. As we emit our foghorn bleats, trying to be found by a world we do not yet know exists, a world with the pronouns *I* and *you*, we must gradually hear a rhythm in the sounds of our escape. That drumbeat is, or it becomes, language.

One life detaches itself from another without any *first*. You might as well say, *the first light of sunrise*—which people do say. But not, I imagine, on a day when there is something at stake in *first light*: the start of a march, the pulling of a plug. On such a day I think I would ask how dark a gray is daytime. Did day come when there was that feeling of a somewhat greater shift in light than all the other shifts? Did it come while I stood up, distracted, to check a lock? Then when it is day, it seems that something so momentous as a day must have had its moment, surely. The greater truth is the one that was visible before, in the midst of uncertainty. There is no present tense for this change. It *will have been* and it *was*. But it never *is*.

On the day when my children were born, the doctors drugged me extravagantly. First it was Tylenol in paper cups, then Pitocin by IV, then an epidural, punctured through the base of my spine. The source of the drugs moved from my twelve to my six, from my mouth to my spine, as if in ritual recognition of my vanishing control. After the placing of the epidural, no one bothered to name the drugs anymore or even to signal their coming. So harpooned, it was not clear to me in which ways I could or could not move, what would pull out this invisible but highly consequential tether. Bewildered bulls may feel the same, led by rings in their noses; or whales, pierced by a blade at the end of the rope that leads to the whalemen. You can guide a great beast if your guidance also threatens to tear his flesh unpredictably. It is possible to be born with your spine reversed, on the outside of your body; it is possible for a mother, in the throes of childbirth, to break her own tailbone with the force of her bearing down.

Because I was having twins, I was to deliver in an OR. Everyone kept warning me about this fact, but they did not know how to say what they were warning me about exactly. It will be clinical, they said. There will be a lot of people, they said. These good-natured attempts did not capture the problem. The problem was that I, awake and hugely pregnant, was to be accommodated where unconscious bodies are usually accommodated. In the middle of the room there was a metal slab, its top more than waist high off the ground. It had no bars around the sides, no stirrups, no reclining back. I suppose I was lifted onto the slab; I couldn't have climbed. I think I was given a pillow. For stirrups, one resident held each of my feet. The anesthesiologist spoke to me as if he were a rafting guide and I were a teenage girl on vacation. "Are we ready to do this?" he boomed as I was wheeled in.

The attending at my delivery made the sort of pacifying small talk that attendings do. Checking the dilation of my cervix with one hand, she probed brightly for my interests with the other. She felt around for a hempen line to bring the babies through. Shakespeare is what she found. I have some verses of Shakespeare memorized, and so did she. I started in on Sonnet 116, "Let me not to the marriage of true minds / Admit impediments," and she said it with me, all the way to the end: "Love alters not with his brief hours and weeks, / But bears it out ev'n to the edge of doom. / If this be error and upon me proved / I never writ, nor no man ever loved."[3] Either the naïveté or the nihilism of the couplet is astounding. He must know, mustn't he, that love alters? Then why is he willfully destroying the world?

My doctor next started in on *Julius Caesar*. Perhaps she was trying to tell me something. My first son was stuck behind a ridge of bone that would not let him pass. Later we would learn he had an injury to his fingernail, the same kind you would sustain if you smashed your hand in a door. Someone, maybe me, gave consent for a C-section. I felt the plunge of drugs like a cryogenic wave, and then I had nothing to do with anything anymore. I saw my first son after his birth but not my second. I saw the clock as they wheeled me out. I watched the strange night nurse hold my breast in her beak-like hand and smash each baby's face roughly against it. I went to sleep. The drug-tide of misinformation took ten hours to ebb.

Athena performed her own C-section from within her father's skull, her war helmet already bristling. Besides Caesar, there was Duncan, and Romulus and Remus, nursed by wolves. What can these myths imply but a disgust at our common origin, from between our mothers' legs? But however we are born, we also crack out of others' heads, like Athena did. In stories our egos gestate, still held between ourselves and others. We make language out of breath and the battering and whistling and wheezing of the mouth and throat and tongue. Then we find our place in it.

To constitute ourselves as single people, singly embodied, we tell over and over the dissolutions we have survived. *From woe to woe tell o'er*, says Sonnet 30's Shakespeare, luxuriating in his losses.[4] My sons' first act of narration was to tell over their woes. In the recounting, sadness and pain gave way to intellectual eagerness. They narrated even when they couldn't yet speak with their voices, when they had to run from one place to the other to show what had happened. Their first story told how one of them had thrown up on the carpet in two spots. They would run to the first spot, grunt, and point excitedly at their stomachs and mouths, then at the carpet. Then they would run to the second spot, and do it again. They manifested all the urgency of a Lassie bringing rescuers to the well.

Snake, snake, snake, went another story. *Dead. Broken. Zeke. Mama. Shovel. Shovel. Shovel.* They needed me to fill the grammar in. *Snake. Snake. Snake. Broken. Dead. Mama. Shovel. Shovel. Shovel*, they would keep saying, with an indescribable avidity, until I did. Our husky, Zeke, killed a lizard in front of them, then left a snake carcass in the yard. I picked the snake up on a shovel and threw it over the fence. *Dead*, one would pronounce, squishing a beetle.

There were no pronouns at first, and when the pronouns started, my children did not know that pronouns are relative to the speaker's position. They spoke of the world as the world looked from their parents' eyes. "Me do it," they would say, pointing at their father or me, if we suggested that they could pick up what they had dropped for themselves. "Carry you," they would demand, their hands reaching up to us.

There was a moment of crossover when they still used *I me my* and not *you your yours* for their mother, but they had also started to use *I me my* for themselves. At about the same time, they took an interest in pregnancy. "Story bout I was in my tummy," one of my sons said. "I put my hand on me. Then I got big and I came out." It was true. I was in my tummy. I put my hand on me. Then I got big and I came out. And then *I* was *you*.

how to milk

You might remember the human farm of *The Matrix* as a nightmare of perpetual amniotic suspension. That is how I remembered it. All the people, from babies to adults, umbilically connected to the great machine that feeds on them, look like nothing so much as fetuses that failed either to be born or die. After I nursed my children, the milkiness of this fantasy struck me anew. They are being milked, the *Matrix* humans. They are hooked up to a great vacuum machine that suckles them so that others can feed.

Feeding other beings with your body may be a dystopian nightmare, but it is also a thing that women and other female mammals do every day. During college I worked on a small dairy farm in France—a summer job that didn't pay but that gave me an attic to live in and a chance to learn French (to this day, my vocabulary skews toward the agricultural). We milked the cows once in the morning and once at night. They were compliant, even eager for the relief that milking would bring them. More often than not, they would all be waiting at the door of the barn at milking time. If we were late, their udders would be hard with engorgement. I do mean hard, like the smooth wooden knob of a banister. They would come in anxiously, sniffing their way to their own stalls as surely as if they could read the nametags lettered by hand over their mangers: *Étoile, Framboise, Luna, Pepsi, Tilleul, Sureau.* I would hitch their bridles to a steel bar and spread the grain on the floor in the front of each one. Multipasse, the gray tabby, threaded among their feet scouting for spilt milk. The chickens wandered by and idly pecked the grain. Sun slanted in from the east door to the vegetable garden, or from the west door to the field, depending on the time of day.

To milk them, we used vacuum pumps attached to a central air compressor. From the compressor, vacuum tubes ran down from the rafters of the barn to each of the eighteen milking machines. Each machine consisted of four steel cylinders lined in rubber that would compress and expand around the cow's four teats with the suckling of the central vacuum. Before connecting the machine, I hand-milked, squirting a fine jet into my palm from each teat to check for the small grains in the milk that could indicate tuberculosis. Then I held one flange after another carefully under the udder until, with a sound like a household vacuum fastening onto a sock, the flange sucked the teat in. Hanging from the cows' udders, the machines resembled candelabra.

Milk collected in another set of tubes and poured into a ten-gallon steel pail. This we would carry to a clean room adjacent to the barn. A two-hundred-gallon steel cooling vat took up most of the room, its gyre swirling the milk in silken folds past some hidden refrigeration element—whatever moved and cooled the milk, you couldn't see. Gallons upon gallons, from eighteen cows, hot enough to steam when poured out of each aluminum bucket we brought from the barn, had to be cooled within minutes so that the milk could safely stay raw for cheese. Beyond that room was a series of rooms with cheeses in baskets, the *tommes*, or wheels, getting yellower, harder, smaller, older, with each successive stage. Sometimes we set a little milk aside to drink with our coffee. I scalded it in a saucepan to pasteurize it.

One can also harvest human milk by vacuum tube. The technical differences between a breast pump and a milking machine are not enormous. A breast pump looks something like the earliest cellular telephones, a heavy block of machinery carried in a nylon bag. My pump was butter yellow. It consisted of a machine for compressing air, vacuum tubes leading to flanges that connect to the breasts (two cone-shaped flanges for humans, where there were four cylindrical ones for cows), and small bottles for collecting milk (a few ounces for humans, many gallons for cows). Tubes and cords and tethers seem to be everywhere: tubes for the vacuum suction, tubes for collecting milk, cords for electrical power. You have to remember not to stand up and disconnect the tubes, break the seal, spill the milk.

In the first weeks after my sons were born, when I came home from the hospital, my milk wasn't coming in and they weren't nursing well. One of the nurses taught me to hand-express milk into a spoon and feed it to the babies. My efforts yielded about enough matter to fill the corner of an eye. I was frantic about it, in ways that are not easy to reconstruct now. To increase milk production, I pumped while I ate, while I read, while I wrote. For nine months I pumped every two to four hours, around the clock. I labeled milk, I froze milk, I pumped at work and at home. I picked figs after dark with a flashlight because, after putting the boys to bed, I had to pump before I could do anything else. Every time they woke up in the middle of the night, I nursed them, then went to pump in the other room.

The milking technology for cows is in many ways superior to the one for humans. Their first advantage over us is that they walk on all fours. Thus the dangling of the teat, the direction of milk flow out of the teat, and the direction of gravity's pull are all the same. Humans walk upright, and so milk flow and teat and gravity are at sixes and sevens. Milk tends to dribble out the sides; you must sit upright; the flanges cannot be held on by vacuum alone, but instead require a special bandeau to strap them to your chest. To pump as a cow would frankly have been more convenient: standing in your familiar stall, with gravity and the vacuum and the long teats deep in the flange all taking the milk in the same direction.

I would sit there at my desk, upright, writing, pumping, tethered to the tubes, with my peanut butter sandwich—my scatter of grain. What I wanted was for my sons to have the feeling of provision, of love, that babies have if they nurse from birth. Or that I imagine that they have—but I have seen these babies, and I think I see what they feel. For a short time I nursed both of my sons directly, one at a time, every time they woke in the night. I barely slept. I had to stop. Something slipped out of my grasp. Four years later, I have never removed the pump from the file drawer of my campus desk. Putting the milking machine on a cow, the verb you use in French is *brancher*, to connect.

Milk is prominent in metaphors of solace: the land of milk and honey; the milk of human kindness. The pelican is an icon of Christ because at some point people thought it pierced its own breast with its beak to feed its young with blood. Jesus, then, would be a lactating man. In the *Pietà*,

Michelangelo's sculpture of Mary holding her dead son, the artist renders Jesus's body in a position as closely resembling that of a nursing infant as his full-grown adulthood will allow. Some Mary sculptures miraculously lactate.

But exploitation is milky in our fantasy lives too. Our use of cows is one such exploitation; we separate their calves from them and take their milk. One morning on the farm I woke to find that a calf had been born in the night. Trembling cannot describe him. Wet, abject, he vibrated in his tripod stance on the straw. One gasped to see life inflict itself upon him. He would stay with his mother for now. She was still producing colostrum, a scant secretion rich in antibodies, yellow as gold, that precedes milk in humans and cows. It is useless for making cheese, which is what we were doing, but useful for strengthening calves. It would be gone within a few days. Then we would trade him his mother for a pen alone and a bottle from our hands. She would go back in the vacuum milking queue. He would cry for her, and she for him. Husbandry requires this.

Our neighbors who raised beef cattle took the animals' lives at the end, but not their mothers at the beginning. Because they did not steal milk, they did not need to build trust. Herders of beef cattle do not approach the powerful back feet twice a day, to branch a machine. All spring you see the new beef calves standing under their mothers, nursing at will. You see them as well as you can from the road or the fence, a hundred yards away. Milking, you meet the gaze of dairy cows from a breakfast table distance. Is it an accident they are lovelier to us? The Jersey, her eyes so hugely alien they become human. The Brûnes des Alpes I tended. The black-and-white Holstein, cow in the primers and books, cow on the pajamas, the puzzles, the toys; cow of cows; till the spotted

black-and-white pattern simply *means* cow. *Cow*, my children
said, pointing to a black-and-white dog.

Lactation affords possibilities for thinking about exploitation and mercy both. At one time *fostering*, or nursing a child
someone else bore, was a common form of women's labor,
both free and, during the centuries of chattel slavery, en-
slaved. Infants a mother nurses freely also need to exploit her,
in a different sense of the term *exploit*: not the theft of labor
and milk, but the simple use of a person—innocent in the
infant's case—without regard for her as an other. Infants are
not in a position to have regard for the other; to ask them to
recognize the mother's need would be to inflict psychic damage upon them. The psychoanalyst D. W. Winnicott thought
that infants needed to discover, from the mother's constant
presence, that she could withstand their aggressive demands
on her. He called the mother who could give the impression
that she would survive—and thus be reliably available—a
"good-enough mother."[1] This impression created a necessary and productive "state of illusion" in the baby, as Adam
Phillips explains.[2] Gradually, only as the infant could tolerate
it, the mother would let her in on the news that the world was
separate from the infant's body; that it might distance itself,
but that it would return. This news must not come too soon.

Winnicott wrote with compassion of mothers; they had to
be only "good enough." And yet the mother's task of temper-
ing the wind to her shorn lamb—even well enough—is not
so easy. Lactation really is difficult for the mother to survive,
just as the baby fantasizes it might be. It is not that breast-
feeding might kill the mother but that she might be so dis-
turbed, so exhausted, by the obliviously selfish demands on
her body as to lapse into regarding the baby as an ordinary
other. She might let slide the mental labor of reminding her-

self that the baby cannot yet manage much separation; she might make reciprocal demands on him. She might be depressed, or hungry, or the survivor or present victim of violence; and then she might not be able to produce the illusion of permanence at all. As Phillips puts it, "If she insists upon being a real person, then the infant or young child has to invent a false self to deal with her."[3] She is to hide that she is a real person! She is to do so *just enough!* Some number of lapses into personhood can be acceptable, but how many? How would one know? I imagine every caretaker does lapse. I imagine every caretaker does insist, from time to time, upon being a real person. I know I did, and do. I lapse. When I think about my failures, I feel the same dreadful wave of nausea I felt in third grade when I was responsible for another girl locking herself in her locker out of sadness. The abyss of myself as a harmful person opens up inside my heart.

Irritated, burping someone, I patted too hard. I refused to be bitten. When they began to bite me while nursing, I weaned them. Not intentionally. Yelping, flinching away, I snatched back the confidence I had formerly inspired. I still flinch, in other ways. Without tact, furiously even, I walk out of the room. "May my milk poison you!" is, as historian of magic Stephen Wilson drily notes, "one of the worst curses in the modern Balkans."[4]

My sons visited a dairy farm with their father at the age of three, more than two years after they were weaned. "I saw a baby cow milking his mom," one of them told me. He explained that the baby cow can't drink too much because he has to save some for later. But milk is not supposed to be this way. Lactation brochures in the OB-GYN's office explain that the more the baby nurses, the more milk the mother will produce. That's if the baby will latch, if you make yourself

available, if you succeed. The baby whose mother does not
succeed in giving him a sense of provision will ration himself,
Winnicott thinks; he will learn too early to taper his desires
to the capacities of others. He will save some for later. My son
described milking this way.

In the earliest days the pump seemed to speak with its
every wheeze. It sounded like a human voice. *Rape her* is what
it said. Of course it was not really speaking; it was, however,
articulating, and those were the phonemes. I was sitting, at
the time, on the nursery's sky-blue rug decorated with clouds,
looking at its awning-striped curtains in aqua and blue, at
two in the morning. I was still on opioids from the hospital. Because of the unhealed incision in my stomach muscles,
I could barely sit up straight enough to keep the milk from
spilling out of the bottles and back over my body. The choice
of words seemed neutral at the time. I would not have agreed
that my hearing this command hissed over and over spoke to
any feeling of violation on my part. What struck me as odd
was the pronoun. Who was telling who to rape whom? No
one else was in the room. Why not an address, *you*? Why not
a confession?

how to step over a snake

Once while walking on a riverside trail, I arrested my step just in time to avoid putting my sandal down on a copperhead. The stroller had already passed over his coil-centered head. This snake was only a baby. I like snakes. Still, I felt a quick horror. I was not thinking of venom; I was not thinking at all. The horror is optical, having already happened in the senses before the psyche kicks in. The work of the eyes is to be on the *qui vive*: on the lookout. *Qui vive* is what a watchman might cry, hearing a rustle in the bushes. Literally translated, it means, *who lives*. Who lives out there in the darkness? What might kill me, what might I have to kill? The eyes must distinguish the living from the dead. Snakes defeat this triage like no other animal. Any number of animals camouflage themselves, lying perfectly still. But nothing comes back to life as fast as a snake does. Mice skitter; turtles lurch into aggravated motion. Snakes have a way of skipping the section of film where they started to move. From one frame to the next, there they are already whipping about in the most light-hearted way imaginable, as if nothing had ever been alive but

them. *Qui vive?* A silence. Nothing lives, so I will live. Now
calling again: *Qui vive?* A snake. Nothing lives but the snake.

Rape has an aboutness the way snakes have an aliveness:
put it in the landscape, and it's as though there were no other
theme in the story but it:

> The jar was round upon the ground
> And tall and of a port in air.
>
> It took dominion everywhere.
> The jar was gray and bare.
> It did not give of bird or bush,
> Like nothing else in Tennessee.[1]

A rape is like nothing else in Tennessee. Dead, it comes alive
and takes dominion; it makes the landscape about itself. How
does a person stop it from doing that? In Elizabeth Hardwick's *Sleepless Nights*, amid letters to friends and sharply ob-
served parties and styptic descriptions of sex, the fact that she
was raped comes up a couple of times, never at a high level in
the pecking order of any sentence. She never narrates it. She
never uses the word *rape* in reference to her own experience—
although she does use it to describe a story another woman,
Josette, would not entirely tell her: "Once over a cup of coffee she told of having been raped by someone in the family
and would not say who it was."[2] Elsewhere Hardwick describes some men on a train who make her remember: "Their
whiteness reminds me that they are truly my brothers, going
home to my sisters, my sisters-in-law. The presence of the
men makes me uneasy; one of them stirs my memory because
of the small chip in a front tooth that brings back a woeful
night on the sofa in a fraternity house."[3] I assume she recalls

the chipped tooth because it was inadmissibly close to her face for an impermissibly long time, but she does not say so.

This man's traveling companion "has taken off a tight shoe and sits for a long time voluptuously staring at his liberated foot," a vacant gaze that brings back, for me, a gaze across the yellow light of a bar bathroom.[4] I was twenty; it was when I was traveling in Greece. He had eyes of the sort that always miss all other eyes. I came to midway through whatever he was doing, and I left or was permitted to leave. Maybe I had been drugged. It is not completely clear to me what happened. Another man's irritation blankly, voluptuously addressed.

When I write, I say to you implicitly, *I have looked, I am looking*, and now—in the command form—*look*. I feel myself losing the authority to deliver this imperative when I tell the story of a man who didn't look at me but who, at the same time, constrained me to see him. I am showing you what, exactly? Myself not being seen? "Goodbye," says Hardwick. "Goodbye? I have left out my abortion."[5]

Was it later that very night that I had sex with someone else? It may have been that night or it may have been another night. It was someone I chose, in a place I chose with some eye toward the poetry of ruins, an abandoned building. Leaving just before dawn, I saw an owl sitting on a telephone wire. It was no larger than a dove, a little Minerva who had not yet taken flight but was about to.

When I ask people to look at things I am really asking them to look at me, a delicate thing to ask. I run the risk of being the one who stares vacantly, assuaging the ache of my own foot at the interlocutor's expense; I run the risk, also, that the interlocutor won't look at me at all, and this possibility counts as my erasure, or my death. In poems that waffle over the desire for immortality, I see both of these fears at once. Wallace Stevens's Ariel, who was glad he had written his poems, decided "it was not important that they survive."[6] Percy Shelley ironizes the command he would like to thunder— "Look on my works, ye Mighty, and despair!"—by inscribing it on a colossal ruin, in "Ozymandias."[7] John Keats wrote his graspingest poem on a scrap of paper somewhere—the sort of paper it is not important to save. In the poem, which is untitled, he confesses that his desire for immortality is a wish for the other's blood:

> This living hand, now warm and capable
> Of earnest grasping, would, if it were cold
> And in the icy silence of the tomb,
> So haunt thy days and chill thy dreaming nights
> That thou wouldst wish thine own heart dry of blood
> So in my veins red life might stream again,
> And thou be conscience-calm'd—see here it is—
> I hold it towards you.[8]

The poet who tells you openly that he wants your blood is giving you all the evidence you need to use against him. He is giving you the chance to refuse to look, even as he says, *see here it is.*

"The chart of life must be brought up to date every morning," wrote Hardwick, defending her demand that you look on her works. "Patient slept fitfully, complained of the stitches in the incision. Alarming persistence of the very symptoms for which the operation was performed. Perhaps it is only the classical aching of the stump."[9] The command *look at me* is also a command to look at my world. The patient's symptoms, phantom signature of a long-ago injury, also map the terrain where the injury occurred.

What is not said in the myth of Narcissus is that just before the story began, he had been raped by one of the gods. Such things are not uncommon, after all. He fled to the lake because he needed to take a look at the face that had not been seen. But as he sat, he saw that there was more in the pool than his own image. Beneath his reflected face—only a mirage, after all, and it didn't interest him for very long—there was a real shadow, cast by his real head. Into the shadow some bright silver fish had swum to take shelter. He watched them poised, motionless, balanced, secure. Narcissus didn't move, it's true. Not for the reason that they say. He saw the fish were comfortable there. He wanted to let them stay.

how to herd

There is a poem you surely know. But you may not have thought all the way through the wild utopianism of its gambit. "Baa, baa black sheep / Have you any wool? / Yes sir, yes sir / Three bags full." To ask the sheep for his wool, in English! To have him count it out and hand it over, already in the wool-sack! You speak to the sheep in his native bleats for the first two lines, then he speaks politely to you, in your language. He calls you *sir*! Translation is no problem. Neither is shearing, neither is pastoral care, neither is scarcity.

This is precisely what shearing sheep is not like. Real sheep are ornery. *Ornery* means contrary, cussed. It is a word I used to hear all the time among my cousins in rural Iowa; rarely in urban Iowa, where I grew up; never in the east, where I have lived since I was sixteen. We called people ornery sometimes, if they were mischievous, difficult, or mean, but all these were derivative senses. *Ornery*'s original setting is the handling of livestock. It describes thousand-pound bulls that refuse to move or waves of sheep surging off in the wrong direction, uncontainable by human hands.

Herding is essentially the following conjuncture: you need

an animal to move; you are physically incapable of moving that animal; you and the animal do not share a language. *Ornery* is one of several words for *intractable* that comes from the experience of these standoffs. People can be bull-headed, mulish, and pig-headed. *Stubborn* first meant *untamable*. *Headstrong* refers to a horse who tries to lead one way with its head while you pull the reins in the other direction. People can be said to *balk* because cattle balk. English words for the intransigence of the mute world are husbandry words. The joke of *herding cats* has become necessary only because fewer and fewer Americans have any direct experience with how impossible it is simply to herd sheep.

Looking at sixty sheep bumbling around a pen and treading the mud and shit under their feet into a slurry, asking yourself how you will shear and mark these sheep one by one (you will grab them by the feet; your son or daughter will brandish the electric clippers about the desperately squirming body, nicking the skin; the filthy wool will fall away in sheets; all this will be nothing to get fussed about); you might start to get ahold of what *ornery* means. When I visited my uncle's farm as a child, I watched him shear the sheep with my older cousins. I stood in borrowed Wellingtons safely beyond the fence. The turbulence and violence of it astonished me, but I should have been more astonished than I was. It looked impossible, and it was much, much harder than it looked. On the rare occasions when someone gave me a gate to open on cue or some other tiny job, I saw how incapable I was—saw "a certain self-adjusting buoyancy and simultaneousness of volition and action" that I didn't have—and knew I could have stood in shit until the cows came home and never once caught a sheep by the foot the way my uncle did, sixty times in a morning.[1]

Yet *ornery* does not always have the drama of panicky sheep; it is not always as towering as a bull. These images are yet too sublime, although the experiential knowledge of their possibility is the backdrop for orneriness's calm stand-off. *Ornery* is also the word you use when there is no difficulty about grasping the animal in your field of vision, even touching her with your hand, but there is absolutely no way you can work your will on her. Ornery is a single placid cow who, when you chivy each of her hooves, picks them up and re-places them in exactly the same spot, one by one; who, when you go at her face, tosses her head but otherwise maintains her mountain pose.

I knew an ornery cow once, when I worked on the farm in France. Étoile was an unusually rich sable brown, the easiest of the whole dairy herd to identify. She did not respect the pecking order. In a herd with a bull, the bull is the leader. But a herd whose members are all cows will have to establish a leader through negotiation since sex alone is not disposi-tive. It amounts to a question of who can hold the line, and who wants to. The cow who can best race to the front, then charge any pretenders back, will be the leader. Once estab-lished, she walks at the front of the herd and the herd will-ingly follows. She is sometimes called the bell cow because it is only necessary to attach a bell to her neck to know where all the others are. For pragmatic reasons, a cowherd will prop up the lead cow's regime. It is much easier to control a herd with an intact organizational structure: if you can convince the leader, the rest follow.

In our herd, everyone had settled on a bell cow. I don't remember her name. I remember instead the cow who did not accept the herd's decision: Étoile. She would gallop up the side to charge at the leader, whom she could balk but not unseat. This balking was a problem. When the leader balks, the whole herd takes alarm. They head off in their individual directions. You are dealing now not with a herd but with eighteen individual cows, each weighing around fifteen hundred pounds.

We, the four human beings and the two sheepdogs, one a failed sheepdog, did not want to deal with eighteen individual cows while we moved the herd from the high pasture, near the barn, to the low-lying one by the river. So it was necessary to frustrate the ornery Étoile in her aims and objects. This was my job. No one said how to do it. By lunging, I decided, when Étoile tried to steal a base. I remember the peculiar sensation of being known by her only as an obstacle, not as a mind with a contrary project. She looked at me, but at the same time, she did not look at me. I would lunge; Étoile would charge around anyway. Then the failed sheepdog and I would recede, irrelevant, to deep left field.

The failed sheepdog was a Rottweiler mix named, for some reason, Yucca. He was my particular friend. It is wonderful what a good sheepdog can do but also disturbing; I couldn't love the good sheepdog, Lena, a border collie. She used to herd recreationally. I would return from market to find all the cows jammed in the corner of the fence. Lena had been practicing. She was driven to drive other animals before her—but drive those animals where? She didn't know. Canny as she was, she had no way of setting bounds to her own actions. Without a fence, she would have driven them and herself to damnation. I loved Yucca for his inability to understand this pursuit. He and I once nearly drowned each other, trying to save each other from drowning in a river. I can swim, he could not; but he followed me into the water anyway.

As to Étoile, hers was the kind of refusal that you know, even as it enrages you, is no more a refusal than a wardrobe's failure to budge when you try to pick it up. True, the animal does have its will. But what it doesn't have is any concept of *your* will, nor even that interest in your projects, however mercenary, which is the basic requirement of all human-animal working relationships. A dog or a horse will read you, however little they sometimes know what to do with the peculiar vibe you're giving off. But a cow only wrinkles her skin, cussed thing.

Here is the surprise about *ornery*, though: *cussed* is the one thing it is not. The two words mean the same thing, approximately, but in their histories they are directly opposed. *Cussed* is a dialect pronunciation of *cursed*—that is, from hell. *Ornery* is a dialect pronunciation of *ordinary*—from, that is, this ordinary, daily world.[2] Orneriness is no special upwelling of hell, no Leviathan. It is this world as it is. The ordinary is ornery. You have to get used to that somehow. And if you can—if you find a way lightly to tolerate the recalcitrance of the world—then you might find your way to the pastoral, a genre of poetry that dwells in the golden pauses that good caretaking can sometimes fashion. The conceit of the pastoral is that when the sheep are contentedly grazing, the shepherd sits down in the shade of a tree to sing a poem with his lyre— often a poem about his love for a shepherdess. This marvelous young man unites a capacity for erotic idyll with an ability to wade through shit and truss up sheep—but the latter is never mentioned, only implied by his profession. He is "amative and uninhibited, rascally, gracefully intelligent, highly literate, musical, fit, unself-conscious, curly-haired and beautiful, *and* the capable herder of livestock meanwhile," as the poet Brian Blanchfield puts it.[3]

Meanwhile is the defining adverb of the pastoral: the pastoral happens *meanwhile*, when all is, for the moment, sorted out for the sheep. Think for a moment about the conditions of this rest. The herd is not enclosed in a fence; the pastoral takes place on open grazing lands. The sheep are contained without absolute constraint. They *could* bolt all of a sudden, but the shepherd, with his expert judgment, thinks they won't. Thus the sheep tell him when he may get out the lyre. He can give them a shady glade at the right time of day to rest, but they have to get the notion they will settle there. The shepherd can propitiate these pauses, but he can neither control them totally nor predict them with certainty.

The care of little children also yields moments of the pastoral *meanwhile*. Rested, interested, well fed, not more than halfway through their morning or their afternoon, and thus before exhaustion has started to claim them, my sons will take up some activity and fall into its groove. Usually it is something at once repetitive and accretive: carrying water from a rain barrel to a muddy hole, for example, or burying a toy car under wood chips, or moving sand in a cart, or building a tower. Bent on their labors, they are likely to require little labor from their minders. One can neither choose nor predict when it happens, nor affect it much. At most you fashion a pause. Tapering the energy you give off, lowering your voice, crumpling your body backward and low in the direction you want the ornery beast to follow, you might pacify it. The sheep might settle down to graze. The children might settle down to build a tower. Anything ends it: the scent of a wolf, a wet sock, a property dispute. But until then you can read. You can work elsewhere. Maybe you can even write.

The meaning of this golden form of the ordinary cannot be understood without remembering the other ordinary, the ornery one. The shepherd's vigilant but light heart becomes possible only if he has received the news that the ordinary—

the *ornery*—is not cursed—*cussed*—just because it will not yield to his will. He—no, I—must expect to be dumbly resisted and get to where I can be gentle about it. For domestic care is in large part the meeting of dumb resistance, and this must be done, for the sake of the charges and for the sake of the shepherd, without rage. Now water splashed out of the bath has drained through some invisible crack along the tiles, through the joists of the basement ceiling, and onto the dry laundry. Now the second toy screwdriver is missing and one child or the other is syllogistically, inexorably inconsolable. Now the brass door handle has fallen from the door latch with a clang, chipping all the way down through to the old lead paint on the threshold. Now the three-year-olds are racing naked through the nursery; one has ripped down the blinds and is starting in on a picture book; the other is peeing in the corner—*on purpose*. All this is ornery. But it is ordinary too.

When my children were born, they received Iona Opie's *Mother Goose* as a gift. Many nursery rhymes have a pastoral setting, even if they are not actually spoken by a shepherd. They take place in a world much closer to livestock than the world I inhabit now. In this book, which has since been torn to shreds more through orneriness than overuse, there is, or was, a rhyme I have never seen in any other *Mother Goose* collection:

If I had a donkey
that wouldn't go,
D'you think I'd beat him?
Oh, no, no.

I'd put him in a barn
And give him some corn,

The best little donkey
that ever was born.[4]

The non sequitur is what takes my breath away. No pause to justify the donkey. No voicing of, then responding to, the person who would condemn the donkey. No psychologizing of the animal—he wanted attention, he was frightened. No naturalization of his behavior—as a phase, as what donkeys do. It is not that he is a dumb animal. It is not even that, Christian-like, you will care for him *because* he is a sinner. No: there is simply no reasoning about it. He refuses; you will care and praise. These are the roles that you and the ornery have with respect to each other, the rhyme instructs.

At midnight on the night after we moved the cows, including Étoile, to a pasture that was strange to them, I heard François, who was the head farmer, and the two permanent herdsmen dressing and rushing out the door. I didn't know why. No one called me. The next morning, François told me that the cows had broken their enclosure in the dark. Liberty terrified them, and they howled to have it taken away again. The new pasture was a mile from the house. I asked François how he had known that something was wrong. *Ça guelait,* he answered, which I took to mean, *they were howling.* They were bellowing in terror. Clear as this memory is, I still wonder whether I have misremembered, because why was the subject of the verb *ça, that?* Why not *they?* Did he mean the herd? Or maybe the sound was more to him than the subject. In the night, *howling was. Howling was,* and François came. Howling was; howling was not yet an entity that could hold itself together with a pronoun; howling had no fences to embrace it. François heard them from a mile away, sleeping in his house up the hill. He dressed in a hurry and ran to contain them.

how to riff

Riff has an unknown etymology; it may be an abbreviation of *refrain*, or chorus, the part of a ballad that returns to be repeated between the verses.[1] In blues, jazz, and music that traces its roots to those genres, the riff is a repeated chord progression or set of notes that ties a song together. A guitar riff returns again and again in a song as though to tell listeners where they are, even as the instruments take excursions elsewhere. The song will travel, but it will keep coming back to the riff. Thus a riff testifies to sameness within change.

Riffing could also be described as change within sameness. To say that someone is *riffing* in writing or speech is to say that they are constructing their utterance by starting with a single idea and putting it through a series of changes, embellishing it, making it more and more elaborate and even absurd. Many of the chapters of *Moby-Dick* are constructed as riffs. "The Whiteness of the Whale" is a riff on a question: Why does Ishmael, the narrator, want to hunt the white whale? He is not sure why; trying to tell us, he ends up asking a new question: Why was it that "the whiteness of the whale . . . above all things appalled me"?[2] Again, he doesn't know, or doesn't know how to say, and so his answer to the question takes the form of posing the question again and again, in new forms. Is it not their whiteness that makes the polar bear and the great white shark "the transcendent horrors they are?"[3] Why are Virginia's Blue Ridge Mountains "full of a soft, dewy, distant dreaminess," while merely mentioning the name of New Hampshire's White Mountains brings "that gigantic ghostliness over the soul?"[4] Does whiteness "[shadow] forth the heartless voids"?[5] Is it ghastly, hypocritical, blank?

The mystery of riffing is that it goes somewhere by continually returning to the same place. "The Whiteness of the Whale" keeps asking the same question, and yet the effect is cumulative, climactic. The chapter seems to build to its great final question: With all the horror that whiteness represents, are you surprised that the men wanted to kill the white whale; or, "wonder ye then at the fiery hunt?"[6] It is as though to have posed the question *what is appalling about whiteness* over and over were, ultimately, to get somewhere. Where, exactly? Not to an answer but to a state of deepened familiarity with the social matrix in which the importance of the question is tacitly understood. Riffing signals that the writer is not magisterial. A writer who riffs does not know before speaking the boundaries of the vision and tries to find them through writing.

Sometimes a person can make something by turning words over and sending them back out into the world, when it is not clear what else to do with them. One winter, walking downtown, I saw a neighbor of mine, a man with a cheerfully open face who takes a bounce on the balls of his feet with each step. He is mentally ill. It was a cold day and my neighbor was not warmly dressed. He didn't seem bothered. But two cops approached him to check on his wellness. "How ya

doin'" was all they said, but they had a way of surrounding
him in a semicircle with their bodies and their bikes that in-
dicated he was being detained. It is an essential feature of
greeting someone on the street that as you greet them, you let
them keep walking. This the cops specifically did not do. He
would answer them.

He did; he almost answered back. "How *you* doing?" he
genially replied. He was making fun of them. No; he was guile-
lessly answering them. No; he was using language as though
estranged from it, turning it inside out, following its funny
little rules. He was riffing. How you doing? How *you* doing?
In the end something—his whiteness (he is white), his madness, or his riffing—left them disarmed. They let him pass.

A friend told me that as her mother sank into dementia,
there was a period when she could still converse but had lost
most of her memory. The memory loss meant she could not
supply information or make sense of the information her interlocutor offered. Instead, she would pun on whatever her
visitor last said, taking the words and presenting them back in
an altered form. She riffed.

My sons learn language, and for that matter the nature of
their world, by riffing together. If development is a succes-
sion of interests whose shorthand could be answers to the
question *how am I seeking to use the world now*, then my sons
have always seemed to be seeking to use the world in similar
enough ways that they have a great deal to talk about and
do together. Each will repeat any action that the other has
just done. Twin A coughs because he is sick; Twin B, not sick,
simulates a cough. Twin A breaks a branch from the hazel-
nut tree; Twin B, inevitably, will do the same. Twin B cries
over the loss of a snail shell he had found and crushed; Twin

A mimics the sound of his cries, soon working his way into actual sadness. Twin B runs up a particular stone path saying, probably by chance, the nonsense syllables "hadiyady;" Twin A repeats both the motions and the syllables. This activity is known, henceforth, as "hadiyadying," even when a mourning dove does it. They point to the dove and say, "he's hadiyadying." The path is called the hadiyady path.

These repetitions can extend into a game that seems to dilate time. Especially when the activity is both repetitive and accretive, the two of them can become intently, joyfully suspended together. It happens, for example, in a game they call "building a fire," after the experience of bringing and arranging kindling for their father's wood stove. They build a container from their blocks, then run with purpose all through the house, finding things to stuff inside (their socks and underwear for paper, blocks and books for logs). The act of stacking joins a stacked language: "and we put another one on there," says one; "and we put another one on there," says the other, over and over, with the same prosody and melody each time.

Sometimes the nature of the repeated act will unobtrusively shift. I can compare this process best to a song structure like that of Steve Reich's "Piano Phase," a piece for two pianos in which the shifting and mutually responsive tides of the two instruments recall electronic music. Two simple patterns, one played by each pianist, slip in and out of phase with each other. Things shift; without there being a definable moment of change, the pattern is no longer the same one. It is as if the first player's hands gradually recruit some extra notes to themselves while dropping others, until the pattern becomes fully what you could sense it was leaning over to

become. It *resolves*. But it does not resolve some unitary problem. It isn't that the pianists were operating under an illusion
in Phase 1, and now, in Phase 2, they see things as they are.
No; attachment to Phase 2 is also not the point. It, too, will
fall out of phase to be replaced by something else. The song is
of variable length because, as the performance directions in
the score indicate, "the number of repeats of each bar is not
fixed . . . . The point throughout . . . is not to count repeats,
but to listen to the two voice relationship and as you hear
it clearly and have absorbed it, move on to the next bar."[7]
These shifts never happen, and they are never not happening.
No one of them is more or less important than the others.

Riffing can construct. You can return over and over to the
paucity of your knowledge—to a word, for example, that you
don't fully understand—or to a question that you don't know
how to answer, or to a theme. What to me was the whiteness
of the whale? The gamesomeness of this return is sufficient to
cause something to appear out of nothing. Something cannot
help but appear out of nothing. And thus you can inflate for
yourself a room whose capacity is right. This room would be
expansive enough that the body can move, enclosed enough
that the mind can rest. Then sometimes, others can use
these rooms too, after the writer is finished with them. It is
as though writing can be perceived as an environment. In the
reading of certain writers, many of the ones cited in this book,
my thoughts and annotations in the margins are less narrowly
topical comments on what is being said than records of what
the words have excited. What I thought of while I was in that
room. Riffs.

I did not grow up in any church, but my mother did, and
she sang "Amazing Grace" to me as a lullaby. As long as I can
remember, I have known its timing, its iambic lines alternat-

ing between four and three beats, its strong medial caesuras (pauses) in the first and third lines:

> Amazing grace, how sweet the sound
> that saved a wretch like me
> I once was lost, but now am found
> was blind but now I see.

This is the ballad stanza, or almost; the first and third lines in the ballad stanza do not ordinarily rhyme as they do here. But the timing is the same, and to live in this room—*stanza* means room, in Italian—is something that a great many parts of American culture teach you to do: hymns, country music, gospel music, rock. Once, poetry of diverse kinds might have taught you to live here. In the nineteenth century, broadside ballads reported the sensational news of a murder, an abortion, or a hanging, set to familiar tunes on cheaply printed and widely circulated sheets.[8] Now the poems that first carry the ballad to you are probably nursery rhymes. "Jack and Jill went up the hill / to fetch a pail of water / Jack fell down and broke his crown / and Jill came tumbling after" is a ballad stanza.

I was an adult when I first heard a recording of Aretha Franklin singing "Amazing Grace" live at New Temple Missionary Baptist Church, in Los Angeles, in 1972.[9] Franklin first establishes the time of the ballad stanza by singing a verse through. Then, in a later repetition, she declines to part from the word *amazing*. She begins a series of descants with the first syllable, then on to the second, then the third. You cannot know in advance how long she will carry it off; it is like watching someone on a tightrope crossing a void. Finding notes between notes, she finds seconds between seconds, until time is doubled, tripled, squared, cubed. There is time inside time. She is not walking forward through time toward death, but inward through time to a room. As Franklin delays the resumption of the ballad stanza's three-beat, four-beat pattern, minutes are added to your life. What will you do with them?

how to turn the corner

Light and slim, with little to no vibrato, Blossom Dearie's voice is ingenuous to such a degree that you could wonder whether it isn't, in fact, the least ingenuous thing you have ever heard. It echoes flatly across the foursquare court—or was that the tomb? Imagine the Sphinx challenging Oedipus. Then ditch the immortal growl and hear, instead, a girl. That's Dearie, spinning her riddles of love and disaster. Dearie was an American pianist and jazz singer. Her solo recording career ran from the 1950s, when she released six albums with Verve, almost into her eighties.[1] She was a cabaret regular. Dearie mostly did not write her songs, but she often arranged them, and her ear was inimitable. She knew how to slip a taste of death into a nursery rhyme, and she recognized lyricists who could do the same. Sometimes she chose well-known songs like "Just One of Those Things," but she also gave new ones their debut. Dearie was the first to release the song "I Walk a Little Faster," which appeared on her 1958 album *Give Him the Ooh-La-La*, where Ray Brown played bass, Herb Ellis played guitar, and Jo Jones played drums. The song is about a person who has been unlucky in love,

but who learns nothing from her disappointments. Cy Coleman wrote the music; here are some of Carolyn Leigh's lyrics:
"But even though I meet / at each and every corner / with
nothing but disaster, / I set my chin a little higher / Hope a
little longer / Build a little stronger / Castle in the air / And
thinking you'll be there / I walk a little faster."[2]

The singer of "I Walk a Little Faster" is like "one of those
who," as Elizabeth Hardwick wrote, can "look into new eyes
and say: Now I am going to be happy."[3] Hardwick had men in
mind, the ones who easily find domestic bliss even after years
of bumbling about. She, too, used the metaphor of a corner—
that place rife with intimations of whoredom for women and
of *flânerie* for men. "I often think about bachelors," she wrote.
"A life of pure decision, of thoughtful calculations, every in-
clination honored. They go about on their own, nicely ac-
companied in their singularity by the companion of possibility. For cannot any man, young or old, rich or poor, turn
a few corners and bump into marriage?"[4] If there is delusion
in Dearie's quick walk, there is also the heroism of claiming
the same possibilities at corners that bachelors unthinkingly
enjoy. But one worries about her. What will become of a person who hopes this much and judges this badly? Whose *faster*
keeps rhyming with *disaster*? Dearie plays a thundering trill
on the piano under the word *disaster*, like they used to play on
the silent movie scores when the villain entered the picture.
But then it's chin up; let's race back to the brink; let's walk
around the corner.

When Dearie recorded this song, she was in her early
thirties. She still looked like an ingenue from central casting:
small, white, blonde, cute. Thirty was a little old for ingenuousness, and this was precisely her game: she insisted on
innocence, which is to say, she insisted on *possibility*, past a

woman's youth. Dearie, having been allotted the role of the ingenue by the smallness and whiteness and blondness and femaleness of her person, forced from this condition the last drop, sweet or bitter, that it could possibly give.

Those words echo James Baldwin's, from the introduction to his first book of essays, *Notes of a Native Son*, which was published in 1955, a year before Dearie's first solo album came out. He commented: "One writes out of one thing only—one's own experience. Everything depends on how relentlessly one forces from this experience the last drop, sweet or bitter, it can possibly give."[5] This is, or should be, a fearful piece of news for a white American. The basic psychic condition of whiteness, Baldwin saw, was that of being the author of tremendous suffering but not wanting to know about it, of wanting to live out the stolen sweetness of one's life without knowing it was stolen. How does one write about a sweetness whose reality is bitterness, without claiming any kind of expiation on one's own behalf? How does one reveal the delusion of this innocence without petitioning that forgiveness be granted in honor of one's new awareness—a forgiveness, to recall Baldwin's words to his nephew in *The Fire Next Time*, that cannot and should not ever be given?[6]

If a white woman is to represent her whiteness, one promising idea is to portray an uncanny innocence. This would be an innocence that knows, in some part of itself, that it is not one. The degree of the *knowing* is tricky. The writer must not cross over into revelations of hypocrisy that too quickly empty the innocence of its appeal. The audience must not be bored by the writer's ingenuousness to such a degree that they go stampeding toward the predictable unveilings: behind the placid surface of the suburbs is perversion and abuse; possessing the wide-eyed doll is a demon. They must be taken in, at least in part, by innocence's luster in order to estimate its power aright. Can you or can't you continue to enjoy the lush green grass of *Blue Velvet*'s suburbia even while knowing the shot will end with a whining Dennis Hopper flourishing his scissors around Isabella Rossellini's body as she lies narcotized with fear?[7] The innocence that lets me move on too quickly to repudiation is not the one I need. I want an innocence that is also an irony, a deluded beauty that has not tipped over yet into horror but might still. For that I look to Blossom Dearie's voice.

I think Dearie forced from white American girlishness the last drop, sweet or bitter, it could possibly give. But to do so she had to perform what Baldwin called elsewhere the defenseless fatuousness of the white voice—and how earnestly or ironically she did it can never be finally determined. In *The Fire Next Time*, Baldwin wrote:

> In all jazz, and especially in the blues, there is something tart and ironic, authoritative and double-edged. White Americans seem to feel that happy songs are *happy* and sad songs are *sad*, and that, God help us, is exactly the way most white Americans sing them—sounding, in both cases, so helplessly, defenselessly fatuous that one dare not speculate on the temperature of the deep freeze from which issue their brave and sexless little voices.[8]

Did Dearie have a brave and sexless little voice? It is essential to the promise I see in her persona that she can never be fully acquitted of the charge. It is only because her degree of distance *can't* be determined, because she doesn't permit us or herself a knowing, nimble leap away from culpability, that the extract she makes of American innocence is potent enough to be an efficacious medicine. Her first recording, with the French ensemble Les Blue Stars, might well sound helplessly, defenselessly fatuous to some ears. Like Baldwin, Dearie spent the early fifties in Paris. There, in 1954, she recorded the album *Octuor* with Les Blue Stars, a group she formed at the direction of Eddie Barclay, head of the Compagnie Phonographique Française. One of the songs, "Légende du Pays aux Oiseaux," was a rearrangement, by Michel Legrand, of George Shearing's "Lullaby of Birdland." The Blue Stars' French-language version became a surprise American hit, now again under the title "Lullaby of Birdland"; the single's success led to Dearie's later contract with Verve Records.[9] Les Blue Stars sound like a French-speaking version of the Lawrence Welk Singers. Their harmonies seethe; one can easily imagine them on the stage of the Ed Sullivan Show in pastel-purple outfits all cut from the same bolt of polyester cloth, ballroom dancing with six inches of air between any two bodies. When the hit single came out, it was 1955, the year of the murder of Emmet Till and the start of the Montgomery bus boycott.[10] *Notes of a Native Son* was published. The Americans who bought the single wanted a lullaby of Birdland. Dearie was in this number.

The difference in her solo work, which she began to record in 1956, is that the same innocence begins to sound haunting and unsupported, and the chosen songs begin to dwell on the topic of delusion. Delusion in love, yes; but still delusion. I think there is something to be said for this defenseless presentation of her innocence. It is at once sexually defiant—she claims the right to hope for pleasure as a thirty-year-old woman—and racially undefended and indefensible. There is no assurance of conversion away from whiteness. Nor is the voice shoring up its entitlement with the harmonic

coordination of the Lawrence Welk Singers; it is not suggesting a closed and satisfactory world. I think—I imagine—I
hope—that such an eerie portrait of the white garden finds
a way not to disavow its own false innocence instantly with
a knowing gesture. The bitterness and the beauty both have
to be acknowledged. At the same time, it is necessary that
nothing be put forward on one's own behalf. The voice that
could hold these things together was flat and slim, with little
to no vibrato, floating out over the air.

how to have a one-night stand

A Greek soldier once said to me on a private bunk in a ferry boat, "You are a good whore." I found it absurd. *I* had bedded *him*. I had watched his heavy ingenuity work to overcome the resistance that I was not, in fact, mounting. Who did he imagine was the innocent one here? Who did he think was out-thinking whom? "It's that in their own lack of intelligence they think they see you coming when it's you who sees them coming."[1]

We were in the Dodecanese Islands, a Greek archipelago that hugs the coast of Turkey. The ferry traveled between Rhodes and somewhere I don't recall. I was working, not very hard or well, as a writer for a travel guide. Sex I was accumulating diligently. "In those years I did not care to enjoy sex, only to have it," Hardwick wrote.[2] The men I thought I was having in those days rarely thought they were being had. Clouding this one's mind was his conviction that a naked girl was a bagged partridge. Clothed—well, so long as I had been clothed I had been something next door to a worthy adversary in his mind: sleepless guardian of a thing he wanted to possess. Nakedness was marred, for me, by his sense that he had finished with all that now. Besides the perpetual disappointment of perfectly functional penises of perfectly normal size, there was, worse, the relaxation of perfectly normal intellects from an alluring state of tension into their usual flaccidity. These men lost their quick glory the way a cat loses hers when she unpricks her ears, undilates her eyes, uncurves her paw, lets the dead mouse lie.

I hadn't lost whatever he thought I had lost—which may have been so antiquated an object as my "virtue"—but I had lost something. My prize had been the contest itself. So long as it lasted, we recognized each other as adversary and trophy at once; at least, in a way; at least, I could compel that recognition sometimes. I played love as a checkers match. Checkers, Edgar Allan Poe thought, was the greatest of games for testing the acumen. You might expect chess. Not so. What mattered in chess, he said, was never losing sight of any of the knights' thirty-two possible leaps or of the intercontinental strikes the queens might make on the diagonal. Who was best at keeping all sixty-four squares in mind? People with a certain gift for calculation who had, at the same time, little on their minds to begin with.

Chess favored grinds. But checkers favored intuitive geniuses. "To be less abstract," Poe said, let's imagine a game of checkers "where the pieces are reduced to four kings." How do you win a contest so crude? By the cruelest kind of attack: an empathetic one. In checkers, Poe said, the player "throws himself into the spirit of his opponent, identifies himself therewith, and not unfrequently sees thus, at a glance, the sole methods . . . by which he may seduce into error or hurry into miscalculation."[3] You could win only by using the fact that you were just like the other, in feeling and in thought. Your imaginative understanding of him was your weapon;

your victory evidenced, above all, a humanity equal to his. If you could beat him, it was because you were like him.

More than one of Poe's stories comes down to the following *cri de coeur*: Look at me, predator; I am your fellow beast of prey. Pairs of men press toward each other against their mutual repulsion, like magnets with the same charge. In "The Purloined Letter," Dupin, the original for all fictional detectives, plays with Minister D— a cold game of diplomatic calculation to retrieve a damning piece of correspondence. When Dupin wins, he writes D— a note comparing himself to Thyestes: a husband cuckolded by his brother Atreus, who in revenge serves to Atreus the roasted meat of his own children. What satisfaction for Dupin in this brutality? The satisfaction of being seen by the enemy in the act of out-thinking him. The pleasure of suddenly, like a bolt out of the clear blue sky, jumping his fucking king.

Checkers was picking up the bartender at a tourist dive. You appear to be—in fact you are—alone. Could you be so stupid? Apparently you are. Final call nears and you keep staying; you stay past when he thinks you could possibly stay without Fatal Compromise. You look him directly in the eye. He watches you indulgently as the possible victim of his rape, if he even wants to bother. But as your brazenness worsens, he glances in involuntary panic at his friends. Can it be that he is doomed to fuck you? Now he ducks his head away from you when he opens the door to his walkup; now there is something flinching about the backward hitch of his head. Like a good dog being swatted on the nose, he would like to extricate himself without biting you. You see a picture of what turns out to be his girlfriend. You ask who it is. He snarls, don't you talk about her.

Cruel on both sides? Absolutely, and even with all this

cruelty, no one could quite land on the square they wanted. We wanted to be loved as something other than we were, and then, by the pharmaceutical power of a stranger's regard, to become that thing. We waited, interminably as it turned out, for the stranger to reveal to us what the thing we were becoming was. *Pharmakon*: cure and poison both. But the wonder of it was that as long as the game was on, you could compel a kind of recognition. While they did not yet have you, they had to hail you as possessor of yourself. You played, like anyone, for sex. But then you played also to make them recognize you as a contestant.

I still encounter wars in this shape from time to time. They happen anywhere that two things are true at once: men wish for women to recognize their prowess; and men decline to acknowledge that women might be, even potentially, possessors of a prowess greater than the one they are asked to hail. At a faculty cocktail party a year or so ago, I said my first book was about mesmerism. The man I was talking to commanded, "Tell me why Darnton is wrong." Robert Darnton is the author of an important book on mesmerism in pre-Revolutionary France, though this fact was not explained; the idea was to see both whether I knew and whether I had something to say. He meant both to test and to tantalize me with the vulgar omission of the first name. "Another teacher of women. You haven't read Gibbon? How is that possible, you with such fine legs?"[4] Up surged bloody murder. I said some things at a fast clip: event versus discourse, French Revolution versus secularism, this scholar versus that scholar. Middle fingers all. *Summa cum laude, high goddamned theory.* I was livid; this man was pleased. Turned out he liked a little aggression. He reorganized his features as a stroked cat will do. We should talk more, he said. Let's have a drink, he started to say, before transforming that invitation midsentence into a promise to send his female student to my office hours, she his foot soldier in case I might have my weapons free.

He was right, I did. I felt, above all, cheated: After all my work to please, did the patriarchy really have no fitter representative to send me than this buffoon? Didn't the one supposed to know, know *anything*? Here I was, ready to beat the test as it had never been beaten before. I was killing it. I liked killing it. But the moment the contest was over, the prize evaporated in my hands. What did I get for winning? Only that expense-of-spirit-in-a-waste-of-shame feeling: the zipless fuck of the intellect. I am enjoying myself: (a) a lot; (b) a little bit; (c) not at all. Both (a) and (c).

But I am not here to perform a conversion away from these ferocious games. No; I think the prize they offer, if ephemeral, is still worth having for as long as it lasts. To be beastly in the other's eyes is something to me. It is a form of freedom, an unleashing. And unleashing does not necessarily have a bloodbath as its consequence, as we should know from the animals we domesticate. Sometimes the opposite; sometimes it has a gentling effect. Pull on my hound dog's lead, and he will pull back against you, hard; he will get more and more unmanageable all the time, as he seeks to respond to whatever emergency it is that has made you want to choke him. Let his lead fall loose, and he may take himself to have been released. Now he can sniff around. He will not walk in a straight line or at a constant pace. He will follow scents; trot forward; double back. He is a predator, but his predation does not narrowly revolve around some prey. Before he finds the trace, he senses the high relief of everything. He hears the buzz of a wood bee. His years fall around his feet like water dropping from the body of a swimmer. He tips his head; he bristles with joy.

When he was a young dog, we would go on long walks in the deep forest, where we met no one to complain about his running free. We stayed faithfully near each other, except when he smelled a fox. Then, deaf to me, he would tear off into rough country at speed, crying a deep desirous bark unlike any of his ordinary calls, until his voice faded into silence. My heart went with him. Exhilarated for him, I endured, also, a frantic terror I can still feel like a balloon inflating inside my chest. Somewhere, up that hill, he was crossing a train track. It was possible he'd reach the highway. He was gone, but I kept calling his name at intervals; I could not stop myself. It was not so that he could find me again, when the fox hopelessly outran him, as the foxes always did. He had no trouble finding me. It was so that, while he was gone, I could believe in his return. He always did return, radiant with joy, his tongue hanging out of the side of his mouth. He fell in beside me and sniffed for dead animals as I looked for birds and mushrooms, our hearts hammering in our chests.

The clear pool you can reach by crossing through the tumult of erotic contest is something like this: you become capable of a rapt, unfocused wandering. Locked into the chase at portside bars, I too saw clearly the motions of bees. The violet color of the sky vibrated with meaning. I felt my hand on the martini glass as though it were impossible I should falter. Speaking, I knew as surely what the response would be as an actor does who has read the script of the play. I could experience the clicking satisfaction of correct recitation, even though there was no script, and we were free.

This quality of attention is friendly to aesthetic experience. We remember we are mortal, and we do not yet know enough—we never know enough—about whether we are loved. Every sensation must be gathered up, sifted for clues—which is to say, savored. This is why Poe's greatest portrait of a predator, the detective Dupin, is also his greatest portrait of an aesthete. The eccentric Dupin shuts himself up in a dark mansion by day, reading the rare books he collects, then ventures forth at night, "roaming far and wide until a late hour, seeking, amid the wild lights and shadows of the populous city, that infinity of mental excitement which quiet observation can afford."[5] As Charles Baudelaire wrote of another of Poe's predators, a convalescent who follows a stranger through the city streets, having lately "returned from the valley of the shadow of death, he is rapturously breathing in all the odours and essences of life; as he has been on the brink of total oblivion, he remembers, and fervently desires to remember, everything."[6] He is not chasing prey; he is chasing predation itself, and its nearness to the bleeding edge, where you can sharpen yourself enough to see clearly.

It must be that erotic risk feels to us like the risk of death. As if the withdrawal of the other's regard—even this new other, to whom we have yielded nothing as yet—would leave us as completely shipwrecked as death could do. If I chase you, I have gambled on your regard. In what seem the last breaths I have before the dice fall, I live a whole life, all the life I have left until you look at me with desire.

how to listen

Anne Dufourmantelle recounts the story of an analysis in which the patient can't move on from a love affair. The patient has an abiding passion for a man who has abandoned her. One week she is lamenting as usual. The analyst—not Dufourmantelle, but a man she does not identify—is by this time bored with the patient and is no longer giving her his best blood. He becomes distracted by an especially beautiful pigeon perching on the window. Watching the pigeon, he forgets to listen. The pigeon flies. His attention returns. And he sees that there has been a startling change.

In a new voice, "as if she had climbed out of an immense sadness," the patient now says, "He didn't love me anymore, I think."[1] Nothing in the analyst's experience of the patient prepares him to hear these words from her. She had time to speak only a few sentences while his eyes were turned away. What were the words? He didn't hear. He is afraid to ask. Now, as she speaks composedly of her former thoughts of suicide, no longer consumed by passion, the analyst says to himself "that the bird would never return, nor would she; that he understood nothing, heard nothing . . . that speech can sometimes return all at once and along with it freedom."[2] Only when the analyst understands nothing can something change.

I told an acquaintance the story of the pigeon who lands on the analyst's window. What does the parable mean? I asked. I saw it from the perspective of the therapist. With theory's watchful eye turned away, I proposed, the patient could change her personality. My friend said no: the therapist was not important. The patient, too, saw the pigeon; she, too, was arrested by its beauty, its unheralded landing. The pigeon changed her, directly. Birds are more beautiful when they land suddenly, commuting the sentence of your personality with their swift arrival.

Surprise matters to aesthetic experience, as it does to a cure. To form a taste is a joy, but to *have* a taste imperils the very pleasure that led you to form it in the first place. There I am, liking the sort of thing I like. I have a personality, but do I still have a passion? Have I abandoned the love I had at first, by practicing it?

For those who like that sort of thing, that is the sort of thing they like. The expression comes from Muriel Spark's *The Prime of Miss Jean Brodie*, where Miss Brodie uses it to give a frosty dismissal to those whose tastes she doesn't approve.[3] But one could give this tautology another turn. It might be taken to describe a problem many lovers of art have with themselves. It is possible to be hobbled by our tastes—or by our conscious ideas of them, anyway. Trapped with our ideas of *the sort of thing we like*, we find we don't quite like those things after all—we don't like only them, we don't like them unfailingly. Taste is not a duty we can obey. Nor will it obey us. It wells up from somewhere. It comes in through the side door. It is, at its best, a surprise.

When my sons were two, they learned to open the stereo cabinet. They would twiddle the volume knob around, then press whatever buttons they happened to press—sometimes power. There followed a chemical bleat and some terrible music, Irish folk reels on the worst occasion, besetting me. My sons would wear their look of solemn, affectless absorption.

Once it happened to be opera. The blare was as bad as always. I did not yet know it was music I was hearing when the flesh of my throat thickened. An aria was playing, a soprano voice. I teared up. It all happened in the space of several seconds. I saw that my sons saw me crying. How to explain what this was? *Opera*, I said, putting my hand over my heart. This offering was a perfect Rosetta stone to two-year-olds who had never before encountered the music, the word, the emotion, or the gesture. *Bopra*, they said, smacking their chests happily.

Did it have to be loud, did it have to be sudden, to seize me that way? It helped. I am skeptical of what I love, and of whether I love it or have been pretending, all this time, to be the kind of person who would. I fear I might have put this taste in my employment—routinized it. I think so because I have. As an English professor, I draw a salary for routinizing my tastes in four syllabuses annually. Enthusiasm is my day job. What else could I do but at a certain point become someone, based on the best indications I had of who I was?

I didn't recognize the song my sons turned up to eleven, and having looked up the radio playlist later, I still don't; the list said it was from *Beatrice di Tenda*, an opera I had never heard. But not all framing is a matter of conscious deliberation—or, for that matter, of curatorial knowledge. A life came back in those ten seconds. In the liquidity of the soprano's tone returned the extremity of the first opera I saw, at seventeen or eighteen, after a night of dancing when someone crossed an ugly line; after an early morning train ride with my best friend from college, from Boston to New York; hung over, chastened, cold; after a walk through the Met's blazing red lobby; after all those things came the opera itself, the black fabulous beauty of the *Tales of Hoffmann*, suspended all around us in the dark, the squalor of the twenty-four hours before balled up in it as if in velvet, and transformed.

Ever since then, my love for opera has been of an intensity that makes me doubt. Surely this time, whatever it is will not be there. But opera speaks with an airhorn: telling you to take your seats, warning you it will go on whether or not you do. Gilded, tapestried, appointed, opera's lavish outlay defeats my equally lavish outlay of self-doubt. The puffy red-carpeted stairs of the Met in New York shush me; its art-deco crystal chandeliers a few feet too close to the floor promise never to ask if I still love them; the hot high air of the foyer blazes with its confidence that I do. In *Lucia di Lammermoor*, they had a real Irish wolfhound. I am not too good for such ceremonies of waste and expenditure. Opera's blare gives a balm that a reserved art form, one that knows I know that it knows that we are playing, would not be able to give me. Dogged ardor meets my skepticism best.

As for this idea I have that what I love will not surprise me again, Adam Phillips might call it perversion. "We could say that we are being perverse whenever we think we know beforehand exactly what we desire," he writes.[4] Once I saw *La Traviata* at the Met from the extreme oblique angle of first balcony stage right, where sit, I learned that day, the people who own opera glasses and read along with the score. Small desk lamps drop ovals of light precisely the size of sheet music. But you feel like you are peering down a grocery aisle toward the stage—peering cautiously, as if hiding behind the end cap. The soprano's arias cut through my humiliation at choosing bad seats for my father, who was visiting, and I wept, quietly, without letting him officially see.

I am not equipped to solve the problem of my skepticism. Sometimes, though, I am offered resolution. A song alights and fortunately does not know how to hear me doubting it will land. Even a peacock less resplendent than the opera can grant this reprieve; beauty need only come in the form of a pigeon, provided it comes without my will; provided it promises a world that can steal up on me. I have seen and heard thousands of mourning doves in my life. But I would rather look out my window and lock eyes, suddenly, with a mourning dove sitting on a wire than go to a silo where a barn owl is known to live and find him duly peering down at me from a roof strut. George Oppen wrote:

> The inelegant heart
> Which cannot grasp
> The world
> And makes art
>
> Is small
>
> Like a small hawk
> Lighting disheveled on a window sill.[5]

A little interlocutor blows in, not having a hold of much, not being abreast of my long case history in underwhelm. I think of pigeon nests I used to see at the bar across Broadway from the Met, thatched onto the anti-pigeon devices covering the upper alcoves of doorways. The pigeons, not knowing they were anti-pigeon devices, kept house there.

how to have a breakthrough

I also know that you are enduring patiently and bearing up for the sake of my name, and that you have not grown weary. But I have this against you, that you have abandoned the love you had at first.

Revelation 2.3–4 (NRSV)

John wrote the Book of Revelation in a cave on the island of Patmos. One of the islands of the Dodecanese, Patmos is small and rocky, its coast scalloped with sandy coves. It lies like an hourglass oriented north-south, with a narrow strip of land at sea level connecting the two bulbs, on either of which is a hill. The northern hill is mostly open country, with steep roads descending to empty beaches all the way around. On the southern hill is the acropolis. The acropolis of Patmos lacks a temple. A stone city once used as a fortress in case of maritime attack occupies the highest hill instead. These days, some people live in the acropolis and others live in the port, where a person can also drink retsina in the evenings and recover with a Nescafé frappé in the dead calm at two the next afternoon. The whole island is small, and if you were sitting drinking with your back to the acropolis, on one side of the harbor, you would make out clearly, across the swimmers and the sailboat, the arid rocks of the other hill to the north.

The Revelator's cave, a holy place for the Greek Orthodox church, lies partway up the hill on the acropolis side. The cave is less a cave than a low declivity cut out of the arid, scrubby hillside, the kind of place where a snake might shelter from the heat at midday. Here, John prophesied the end of the world, meeting the command of the visiting angel with a sword in his mouth: "Now write what you have seen, what is, and what is to take place after this."[1] Like the sacred spring at Lourdes, the cave attracts pilgrims, and it has been built up with stairs, railings, roped-off paths, and entry gates. Following in a line of visitors, you come down a narrow set of stairs clinging to the rock. All this time the cave is hidden from sight, until finally, at the base of the stairs, you make a sharp turn.

Now you discover that the whole place shines. Someone has decided to gild it, in honor of the saint. Metal covers the walls, the floor, and the shelf where John slept; etching marks the spot where he laid his head. Many holy sites of the Greek islands guard reliquaries and ossuaries, bejeweled gold boxes that house tiny desiccated pieces of saints' bodies. Here a shred of skin, there a finger bone. Standing in the cave is like standing in a reliquary. The relic is the empty space you inhabit. The relic is John's writing room.

Enshrining the profane bits of bodies and worlds is idolatry, according to the Protestant tradition in which I was raised. To accuse someone of idolatry is to say they have mistaken the work of human hands for the presence of the sacred. They think they are worshipping a god; they are actually worshipping a statue—or, in this case, a room. John's cave is an idol to the patron saint of writing, a golden calf of inspiration. So the iconoclast might complain, anyway.

But what is gilding but an honest acknowledgment that none of us are free to leave our revelations alone? If my revelations matter, if they stand out from the rest of life, then I will have to return to them. I will have to work them over, whether with metal or with thought. This is all that the gilded cave said. It said, come! It said, here! In this place, God spoke to John.

At the same time the gilding guaranteed that the original epiphany could by no means ever happen again. No second John could come to write. Everything about the space prohibited any further event. The cave was marked so thoroughly that it could never be marked again. You could not, therefore, complain that something had failed to happen to you; happening, you had been clearly warned, was finished here. You could not say, "is this all?" because it was by virtue of the gilding always *more* than all—and less than all, too, because the real all, the stone the saint's head had touched, was safe somewhere under the metal, sealed forever against being touched again by human hands.

What might have appeared to be an unseemly trumpeting was in fact a flash of profane metal against the profane glance, a sign against a sign. Gilding is *apotropaic*. An apotropaic image is a charm, often hung by a threshold or painted by a door, to turn back evil. Such images are usually frightful; the idea is that by representing evil, one ensures that evil, meeting itself, will turn away. All over Greece apotropaic images hang from key chains, blue bulls'-eyes called *evil eyes* that are meant to repel envious glances.[2] At John's cave, visitors have left votive offerings all along one wall. Many of them are evil eyes, turning away the glance of the bored and the underwhelmed. The gilding, too, works this way. With its flash of counterfeit lightning, it prevents the unfaithful from seeing anything, and also from seeing nothing. It pre-blinds them. The movement of their doubt cannot so much as begin.

The evil I wanted to deflect the first time I visited John's cave, when I was twenty, was the deadening of love. I was not in love, but I expected to be. I planned before then to have had enough sex with enough people that I would have mastered desire. I would have tasted all the adventures of crossing over to touch a stranger; I would have tasted them a hundred times, and I would see that every time was the same as every other. Then I could safely get married. Temptation would no longer tempt me. Reason would weigh the value of new particleboard against old stone, and I would choose the stone. Choosing the stone would be easy.

Love was not what I thought love was, and time was also not what I thought time was. You can no more still desire than you can live the years in advance, which is to say that Patmos is not an hourglass shape like I described. That is what I remembered, but when I looked at a map, I saw that there is an additional, difficult-to-access lobe to the far south, called Psili Amos. I had forgotten Psili Amos. I didn't go there on my first trip. The first time I went there was on my second visit, and by then I was no longer accumulating sex. I was in love with John, a revelation. We got together in Boston, after I returned from Greece. Almost the first time I went to his apartment, he brought out his guitar unasked and sang. I could not believe the audacity of playing unbidden. Irritated, ruffled, I fell in love. If I am ruffled, it has always meant he can steal up on me and move me to tears. Certain songs that he plays make me cry every time, even though I know that they make me cry every time; even though I do not think a person should ever permit themselves to be reliably moved.

I took John to the Dodecanese a few years after my first trip and not long after we met. This was when I saw the third lobe of the hourglass, Psili Amos, a loop inside of time. We rented a moped and rode to a deserted beach. There are pictures of us standing on the cliffs above. I remember the pictures as having a rainbow in the background, though this may or may not be true—it does not sound true. I am reluctant to check. I had ridden mopeds all over the Dodecanese before, always sitting behind a man, and I was never afraid. I burned my leg on the exposed tailpipe of an Italian's motorcycle at the acropolis of Patmos. A blister six inches across formed on my calf. I was afraid of the ugly scar, but never of the mopeds. John is steady. But riding behind him up and down the hills, my palms sweated.

We gilded our revelation, which is to say, we stayed together. Over the first moment of madness and little sleep and Kit Kats for breakfast and mutually fetishizing purchases and the yielding of oneself too fast, not fast enough, we laid and planted. A stone walk, a puppy now middle-aged, an old dog, twin children, bramble patches, vegetable beds. I keep many years' worth of seeds in the subzero freezer. My hobby garden doubles, in my secret thoughts, as our bulwark against apocalypse. John tells me we'll die in any case, when the city water gets contaminated. We go on digging holes for fruit trees. We fill our arms with little cares. Trying to write, I see from an upstairs window that the children are breaking black raspberry canes and cherry branches. I yell to John, who is supposed to be on childcare duty but is instead reading something, probably the early church fathers, on the back porch. He lays the book aside and takes up the work. He seems to be fielding complaints about broken chalk. Everyone is crying except for him.

While the dogs and the children grew, the first stones we

laid for paths became concealed under layers of mulch and violet tubers. I excavated them the other day to raise them back up to surface level. They were still there, unchanged, many in places where I had forgotten I laid them. There have always been times of mulching over and times of digging through, or what Brian Blanchfield calls *near terms*. "With each other physically we are like a couple of elk," he writes of his own love, another John. "There are whole seasons when in our need we get kind of stuck in the lock of our racks and settle for nuzzling. And then, occasionally, a breakthrough, and it can feel like molting might feel, velvety after, and then the good itch for new growth." Then they say, "*we should do this all the time.*"[3]

Locking horns in contest, or patting heads and kissing cheeks with a nuzzling intimacy: this is what we do between breakthroughs. Our aggression toward those we love might seem like a failure. Maybe it seems like a failure, too, to want in effect to repress the passion we feel by making love a place of safety, a downy nest. Only these are not exactly failures. They are where we land when the urgency departs from those words, *we should do this all the time.* The urgency has to depart. I do not want, all the time, to do this all the time. I have other work. I can't just keep bleeding. The scab has to crust over. Taking love to be a contest, and taking it to be a refuge: these are the crusts that let us live with shattering things. They are gildings.

Gold is not the worst thing. It might be as well to go ahead with gilding, but if possible without imagining oneself as solving the problem that one cannot solve; namely, how to hold on to love, or, what is only a different way of saying the same thing, how to prevent new love from coming. What can you do but overwork the metal, and then, when the rococo figurations on the cave have become a bit too much, dig back through until you find your way?

Hooded like falcons, we pass into or out of love.

"What is love? Truly I do not know," wrote Mona Van Duyn in "The Stream":

> Sometimes, perhaps, instead of a great sea,
> it is a narrow stream running urgently
>
> far below ground, held down by rocky layers,
> the deeds of mother and father, helpless sooth-sayers
>
> of how our life is to be, weighted by clay,
> the dense pressure of thwarted needs, the replay
>
> of old misreadings [. . .]

Van Duyn's poem ends with this groundwater breaking up through the cladding crust, right where a dowser stands with a forked rod, having given up her quest: "Here at my feet I see, after sixty years, / the welling water—to which I add these tears."[4]

Defeated and perplexed, no longer trying, turned back by the gilding she has laid down, the dowser finds water. She could have said that getting caught in the rut of her daily life deprived her of breakthroughs. She could have said that the constant burr of the humdrum dulled her. But it is just as true to say the opposite: when she is bored and inattentive, distracted and somewhat depressed, expecting nothing, she finds the spring.

how to love

I was awake when the ambulance drivers came. I felt that they thought I shouldn't have called them. It is difficult to know when to switch over to the word *emergency*. Ashamed that I had used this word at all, I was also ashamed that I had not used it earlier. When should a thing get a new name? Words don't shift with things but blast their reveille all of a sudden, belated and overblown.

An acceleration had taken hold of me and was calling out for a name. I was already bleeding at an astonishing rate, ditching a tampon an hour; then the bleeding started to increase. You feel acceleration in an airplane that has been cleared for takeoff. You feel it, though you might not know you do, every spring, a little over halfway between winter solstice and spring equinox, when it isn't just that the days are getting longer but that they are getting longer by a great deal more each day, as much as two and a half minutes at a time. Each year I go out in a rush and sow peas.

As my bleeding, already fast, got faster, I had a feeling for the curve I was on. My sons were just about one. I took them upstairs, thinking that if I grew too weak, I might have time to put them in their cribs before I passed out. Then I changed my mind, took us all downstairs, and unlocked the door so the ambulance drivers could get in, if ambulance drivers there were to be. I settled finally on putting the babies in their cribs upstairs, crawling downstairs myself, and waiting by the door.

The drivers came, then John came and the weight of judgment no longer rested with me. He sent the drivers away and took me to the hospital himself, babies in their seats. When he was a child, he and his older sister found a wounded baby rabbit. She told him to stay with the rabbit while she went to get help. Then she forgot. When someone found him and his rabbit I don't exactly know. But I know he never deserted his post. He stayed there—this part I am adding, he tells me; I have conflated a few stories and fabulated this one—he stayed there, as the twilight started to fall, until at last his mother wondered where he was and came to find him. He is still the same way.

When you walk along a mint-green hallway to the ER or sit on gray plastic chairs or talk to a receptionist behind glass, you know you are the public and that it is only impersonally, through this fictional medium of the public, that anyone is accountable to you. I waited where they told me to wait, at a little triage station behind a curtain. A resident I remembered from when she helped to deliver my babies a year before came in and told me you can lose a lot more uterine blood than you would think before passing out. This was clarifying. She asked if I was pregnant. I said I couldn't be. She nodded and did the test anyway.

Because you can safely lose a lot more uterine blood than you would think, it took a while for triage to sort me to the top. Sitting on the hospital bed, I bled as politely as I could, down through all the pads and tampons I had brought, through my pants, along the table, and onto the linoleum floor. From my bleeding-room I could hear two doctors catechizing a man across the nurses' station from me. He was trying to convince them of his sanity. They were trying to convince him of theirs.

When the attending came, he proved to be a handsome and humorless person of high-school quarterback build. His blue eyes were slightly widened, as though he were perpetually feigning not to have heard the slur someone had just uttered in his presence. He said I was pregnant. I felt a momentary jolt of elation. Then I started to cry.

Leakages of affect around the edges of a sharply defined, only partially pastoral job—medicine, his job, or college teaching, mine—are often a nuisance. Stage business helps one to get through it. I tend to offer a box of tissues. He offered a portable ultrasound that he wheeled around the bed, showing me the gestational sac sitting low in my uterus right next to my failed IUD. *Yes*, he replied, with an irony he did not entirely succeed in suppressing, when I asked if this situation was dangerous to the baby. By *baby* I meant that I did not know the fetus was already dead.

"I'm probably having a miscarriage," I told my husband when he came in for a few moments from the waiting room, double stroller jamming its way through the door. Nothing could have been more demented than the reasonable tone in which I delivered my news. I sounded to myself like a Poe narrator on the gallows, explaining my crime. *True!—nervous— very, very dreadfully nervous I had been and am; but why* will *you say that I am mad?*[1] They sent me for an ultrasound on one of the big machines, not the bedside ones. Ultrasound suites have an atmosphere of wellness, their affluent light diverting attention from the fact that they are, after all, hospital rooms, complete with the standard wall plug-ins in case somebody codes. I troubled this atmosphere when I crossed the suite, blood dripping down my legs onto the floor. Blood drops have a curiously sharp way of landing on linoleum. Right away, each drop leaks thinner, clearer plasma off to the sides. You see how ready the cells are to come out of solution, how gladly they lend themselves to being spun down in a test-tube centrifuge. Across the suite was its private bathroom, where a clot the size of a lemon passed from my body. *Clot* in this case means glistening jelled mold of blood, a meaning of the word known to me only from giving birth and losing these blood-lemons afterward. It was a queasy feeling, letting it go, not being able not to let it go. *Should that maybe stay in,* I thought. But whatever held this blood in as tissue had already failed, like the light traveling to you after the death of the star. Was I supposed to save it, for forensic purposes? I didn't know. I threw it in the trash. Then I apologized to the ultrasound technician for destroying evidence.

Miscarriage in progress, was what the images would later show. With each snapshot the technician took, the gestational sac had moved a little further toward my opening cervix, a Venus completing its transit across the sun.

What I never could get used to was that no one had hailed this possible life while it still existed. I had not wanted or ex-pected a child. But for a long time after—even now—I can't think about my unacknowledged satellite without grief for his utterly forsaken life. Someone ought to have been speaking to him, thinking of him, dreading and imagining what he might someday be. That someone could only have been me. I half-believed he was a child; he was what *would have been* a child, and this possibility had gone unrecognized until after it was gone. To whom was the duty owed, this most fundamental duty of facing each other? To no one, yet; to one who was not, as yet. To one who never ended up being, or not in time to be spoken to.

Lately I have been looking up writers' birthdays to calculate how old they were when they wrote things. I look down on this new interest as narcissistic, numerological. Nonetheless, it persists. I keep finding out that writers of essays I love were also in their thirties at the time of writing. My twenties were roomy enough for all the ages of man; now I can best cope with myself. Two years ago, when I had my miscarriage, I was thirty-seven. Ralph Waldo Emerson was thirty-eight when he lost his young son Waldo; two years later, he wrote about it. In "Experience," he says Waldo's death hurt him too little. His love must not have been enough. We luxuriate in our pain, he says. *From woe to woe tell o'er.* We are willing to "pay the costly price of sons and lovers" only to be sure we are, or were, in contact with the real. But our survival of the blow betrays us as dilettantes in grief, and in existence itself. "Some thing" Emerson says—he means his son—"falls off from me, and leaves no scar. It was caducous."[2] Emerson wavers between blaming himself for having no scar to show and blaming himself for wanting one.

My child fell away from me and left no scar. He was caducous. "People grieve and bemoan themselves," Emerson comments, "but it is not half so bad with them as they say."[3] It was not half so bad with me as I say, was it? I must have wanted something from mourning. I must have grasped at the evidence my grief offered that I would also love my living children as I should, even though I should. I feel it as a chastisement, that parents and children are to be ambushed into loving each other, before they can find out that in truth they do. The mother is doomed to offer her love in the prideful conviction that it's wanted; the child who says it isn't wanted never will be believed.

Like Cordelia, I flee from love's ceremonies. I find it hard to bear the dark secret they conceal: that I desire every obligation they call on me to shoulder, that every rote word I say in them is true. I have no knack for love under these conditions. Yet these are the conditions. It is, as Emerson said, "very unhappy, but too late to be helped, the discovery that we have made, that we exist."[4]

The reader of "Experience" sees Waldo only fleetingly. But Emerson keeps mentioning hypothetical children: "the boy reading a book"; "as new to the oldest intelligence as to the young child"; "in the growth of the embryo"; "the soul is not twin-born."[5] These instances all purport to be merely the illustrations of thoughts. In the vehicles of his metaphors, Emerson lets himself speak of his son. But only sparingly does he call himself *father* in the tenor. By this stratagem he bundles his genuine love past the checkpoint of his feared hypocrisy.

Pause before you try to discern in "Experience" either the sufficiency or the insufficiency of Emerson's grief; pause before you seek to pierce his self-judgments and weigh the true degree of his fault, whether you want to pardon or condemn him. Keep company instead with the grieving father in this most unhandsome part of our condition: that, mechanically, meretriciously, we keep converting our hearts into words. There is something wrong with human beings that we do this, and yet there would be something wronger with us if we didn't. At last Emerson recognizes this double bind as the condition of any human attachment to the world. "And yet is the God the native of these bleak rocks," is how he puts it. "We must hold hard to this poverty, however scandalous."[6] Up, heart, into words.

how to elude your captors

Is your boat also becalmed? I ask the authors of my books. Your commitments made, your loves chosen, did the wind drop? Did you wonder whether you were meant to wait for the next breeze, or whether you should row for your life? "I suppose, as a poet, among my fears can be counted the deep-seated uneasiness surrounding the possibility that one day it will be revealed that I consecrated my life to an imbecility," writes Mary Ruefle. "Part of what I mean—what I think I mean—by 'imbecility' is *something intrinsically unnecessary and superfluous* and thereby unintentionally cruel."[1] This is a fear I have as a critic. I also have it as a parent. In the shadow of catastrophe, was I rinsing out muddy socks? Was I commenting on Melville? In my attitude to these loves of my life, I find the same mixture of conviction and shame. I am devoted. I am embarrassed by my devotion. I cannot help but envision the contemptuous face of the one who sees my idol as a lump of clay.

Suppose a life that might, or might not, be consecrated to an imbecility. What then? What answers are there, beyond trying to answer with a certainty that can never be secured?

I only know how to evade the question, to keep it from arising. To put mattering in the form of a question concedes too much. The question mark's business with me will never be finished. It stands like a cow in the road, uncomprehending, unmoving. "I find that if I really want to say, 'The world does exist,'" comments Stanley Cavell, "the impulse to those words is not expressed by those words. I want a gesture (perhaps poetry, or religion)."[2] If I say "the world does exist," I have implicitly conceded that there could be two views of the case, Cavell explains. If I say, "poetry does matter," I have made the same concession. Then the road is closed to me that was the only one I could take: to say, in that I speak with other people, in that we narrate and pun and joke and use metaphors and idioms, the matter of poems belongs to us. It cannot be cut away without a scar. There is no sense in cutting it off, then trying to attach it again. *Cats have paws. Can't take them off.*

Italo Calvino tells a story, taken from Boccaccio's *Decameron*, of a threatened poet. Guido Cavalcanti, the poet, walks among the tombs by a church, meditating perhaps on death. Suddenly, a gang of rich young men on horseback accosts him. Your life's work does not matter, they tell the poet. It is possible that he is in some physical danger too; their horses surround and block him. But he does not allow himself to be arrested. He says to the young men, "Gentlemen, in your house you may say to me whatever you like," and with that, he places his hand on one of the tombs, vaults over it, and escapes into the night.[3] Cavalcanti avoids their question, but he also turns their question back on them, and with it, their threat. The tombs, he says, are *your* house. *You* are the ones who have consecrated your lives to imbecility. You have a name of being alive, but you are dead. To complete the series

of apotropaic gestures, his name, Cavalcanti, means "riding
on horseback," from the verb *cavalcare*. If it had seemed that
he was on foot and they were on horseback, the opposite is
true. He, the poet, is the more swiftly mounted.

Cavalcanti does not answer the charge that he has "consecrated his life to an imbecility," but he does handle it—with
grace, with acerbity, with a quality Calvino calls *lightness*.
Calvino writes, "When the human realm seems doomed to
heaviness, I feel the need to fly like Perseus into some other
space." He does not mean an escape to a world of dreams,
but rather he means that he "feel[s] the need to change [his]
approach, to look at the world from a different angle, with
different logic, different methods of knowing and proving."[4]
Perseus is the guide for this change of approach because he
carries the horrible face of the Medusa but keeps it hidden,
all the while floating on his winged sandals. Perseus's "power
derives from refusing to look directly while not denying the
reality of the world of monsters in which he must live, a reality he carries with him and bears as his personal burden."[5]
He floats; he may even be accused of evasiveness, of frivolity.
But Perseus does not answer these charges, even if his mute-
ness means he forfeits his reputation as a serious person. To
begin to defend himself would be to introduce defensibility
back into the picture, and with it, the overwrought affects of
self-fortification. With his lightness, he does not answer, but
he does handle, the charge of *not mattering*. Evasion is not
cowardice; it is the only possibility when so much as to pose
the question is to falsify the case.

I like a poem that evades the demand for ultimate mean-
ing, one that will not come to a point. Emily Dickinson's "A
Bird, came down the Walk" declines to culminate in anything.
It is a lovely and exact description of what I have always taken

to be a robin (because of the bird's behavior, and his diet, and also because of his velvet head—the American robin's head is a slightly darker gray than its body, giving it a velvet appearance). The bird comes down the walk; he eats; he ignores the speaker; he flies away. Beyond this indifference of his, little else happens:

A Bird, came down the Walk—
He did not know I saw—
He bit an Angle Worm in halves
And ate the fellow, raw,

And then, he drank a Dew
From a convenient Grass—
And then hopped sidewise to the Wall
To let a Beetle pass—

He glanced with rapid eyes,
That hurried all abroad—
They looked like frightened Beads, I thought,
He stirred his Velvet Head.—

Like one in danger, Cautious,
I offered him a Crumb
And he unrolled his feathers,
And rowed him softer Home—

Than Oars divide the Ocean,
Too silver for a seam,
Or Butterflies, off Banks of Noon,
Leap, plashless as they swim.[6]

In many of her poems, Dickinson switches restlessly among analogies or cuts away suddenly to Beauty, Truth, or Death.

This one stays at sidewalk level. Even the poem's affects are muted, with the exception of the bird's animal vigilance. It isn't clear what the speaker feels about the refusal of the crumb. But the robin is all the way alive. He calculates, he strives, he soars. Human questions of mattering do not matter to him.

Why does Dickinson point out a bird who does such prosaic things—a bird who does not even sing? Birds who sing in lyric poems often seem to hail the poet as a fellow singer. But we see this bird, instead, trying to live: finding his worm, declining to eat a beetle, fleeing from the speaker's offered crumb. John Keats's nightingale warbles continuously across centuries. Walt Whitman's thrush mourns Abraham Lincoln. Dickinson's robin comes up close and gets about the work of surviving. This poem is about watching a series of alien troubles managed and dispatched. If poets are like birds, then on the view of this poem, it is not because they sing; it is because they mind their own business. The poem goes down the walk. It does not know I saw. It does not ask itself whether I think it matters. My doubt will not annihilate it.

The other day I watched a song sparrow perched on the topmost point of my arched bean trellis, feathers on his striped throat erect, his body the trumpet of his territorial call. The entirety of the tiny body became the huge sound. I rejoiced for him; I took a total interest in his interest in singing. In a similar way, I take comfort in walking my hound dog. His is a different world from mine, but one equally organized by keen preferences. Because of what he can smell, areas of grass that seem undifferentiated to me are intensely important to him. Rattled by the passing of another dog, he will carpet the affected area with his snuffling, pulling in the air so hard and quick that his whole snout shakes. Looking back at you from a wild face is striving and a wish for sequence; not, however, a striving or a wish for sequence that is like yours. You can follow along with a different mathematics; you still get to calculate, but not about yourself. It is only because the animal pursues a real project, and not an idle dream, that watching it is a relief.

In such a fragile relationship of unreciprocated watching—things matter to it, it matters to me, I do not matter to it—lies the solace of Dickinson's poem. In this way a poem might be a way to say "the world does exist" without saying it. The poem, like the bird, works, but not for me; it is interested, but not in me. Making no specious promises to balance my accounts for me, the poem has, nonetheless, an obvious respect for its own line items. Its bird strives, but not on the human behalf; it hunts, but not for our quarry. It says neither yes nor no to the balance sheet in which I weigh out my life. Faced with the question of my death, or of my mattering, it turns the question aside and vaults into the air, plashless as it swims.

how to hope

So little cause for carollings
　　Of such ecstatic sound
Was written on terrestrial things
　　Afar or nigh around,
That I could think there trembled through
　　His happy good-night air
Some blessed Hope, whereof he knew
　　And I was unaware.

Thomas Hardy, "The Darkling Thrush"

It is late December 1900.[1] The year and the century are dying, and everything else is already dead. A poet is looking out on a blasted landscape. Then suddenly, a thrush starts singing—hymning, really—in "full-hearted evensong / of joy illimited." The thrush is no longer young. Thomas Hardy calls him "an aged thrush, frail, gaunt, and small, / In blast-beruffled plume."[2] If the thrush were young, then however blighted the whole world might be, he would have reason to rejoice in his own strength. But he has no reason at all.

Either this thrush knows nothing about the world or he

knows something about another world. Either he sings without knowledge or he praises God. Same for Hardy: he goes back and forth. He says he could think there was hope. Does he think so? Well, with hope, who knows? Whether to hope is seldom a question with a cut-and-dried answer. Cutting and drying refer to the harvesting of hay: in the fall, when the nutritious seeds of the grasses have matured but not fallen, it is time to mow the hay, or cut it, and then dry it. This process is a risky one: the hay must be as dry as possible when cut, and there must be a few sunny days after, with no rain, when it can dry in the fields before being baled up. Otherwise it will mildew and rot. You don't always get good luck, and there is not always a right answer about when to mow: you might have to decide, for example, between harvesting too early for the ripening grain but avoiding showers, or harvesting at the right time and risking them.

When Hardy sees the thrush, he is standing in a stubbly field, one that was mowed months ago. The hay is cut and dried. But as to the question of whether to hope? That field never will be cut and dried. Risks of weather, immaturity, overmaturity, when to strike: these accompany us as long as we live.

When we are being blown about, when we are afloat over fathomless depths, when we are not yet dead, in short, things are not cut and dried. And in this state of expectation, it seems to confer a strange but durable benefit to have alien interlocutors like a thrush or a poem. It helps to behold our conversation partner and to oscillate between *he knows nothing* and *he knows everything*; or, *he doesn't matter at all* and *he matters surpassingly*. Maybe what is helpful about it is that in this oscillation, we climb over, and thus for a moment grasp, our position in the middle, which is that hope is neither abun-

dant nor nonexistent; we neither know nothing nor everything; we fight at bantamweight. "A man," Emerson says, "is
a golden impossibility."[3]

In his book *Tact*, David Russell tells a story of the psychoanalyst Marion Milner and her patient Simon, an eleven-
year-old boy who has lost his taste for the world. Milner, who
was part of the same British "Middle Group" of psychoana-
lysts to which Winnicott belonged, helps Simon to take an interest in life again.[4] She describes Simon putting her through
a "ritual catechism which would begin with 'Why are you a
fool?' and I had to say, 'Why am I a fool?' Then he would answer, 'Because I say so.'"[5] Milner remarks on the burden that
Simon bears if he thinks that all adult foolishness is his doing;
there is such a lot of it to be responsible for. I am also struck
by this moment as a meta-commentary on the gift that the
psychoanalyst gives by being willing to say, "I don't know."
Simon needs an interlocutor to agree, "I am a fool." Milner
assents. She offers her foolishness to him.

Offering to be a fool is often a component of care. One
might know better than to be a fool, be stung by it, have a
clever theory about why the other needs to think one foolish,
and so forth. But one keeps these things hidden under an
arm, like the burden of Perseus, and one simply says, *I am a
fool*. Ideally, anyway. My children, now three, have just started
to play catechistic games of Simon's sort. One such game in-
volves pretending to take things from me that I pretend to
want, then instructing me, "let's be sad." I obey and say, "I'm
sad." They'll respond, "let's stick your lip out." I pout. They
erupt in gales of laughter. Then they say, "let's be very, very
sad" and that means I am supposed to pretend to sob. I obey
again. Now they are so seized with hilarity that they often
actually fall over.

Other times they want me to be someone else. My sister and her wife also have twin boys, younger than my sons, and a video of my sister-in-law Josie holding her son Z. and dancing with him made a deep impression. Now they want me to be Josie. "Are you Josie?" they ask. I say, "I'm Josie." "I'm a little baby Z.," they reply. I am sorry that it isn't me they want me to be. But I say, yes, I'm Josie.

I don't know what these games mean, except that they are innocent and at the same time unsettling to me. Do they think that Josie would have held them better? And why do they want me to be sad? Do they fear my sadness? Am I depressed—by the end of the world, perhaps—and are they telling me to play this out in a game? Do they worry that my emotions are something they must manage? If so, I have let them down, maybe calamitously so. Did I fail to hold them together? Was I not, in Winnicott's technical sense, *good enough*? I want and dread to know. I don't know. My avidity changes nothing about my ignorance. Whether the adults my sons rely on have failed in the ways they can tolerate, or not, is something I am blind to. I can only try to play along, imagining, in the spirit of Milner, that they can tell what fantasies they need to live out.

To let us live out our fantasies, to be our fools, is something we can also ask of poems. In the relations that poets establish with birds, there is much fruitful confusion as to who is tending whom. Does the bird consent to be a fool for us, or do we agree to be fools for him? Who is the idiot? That is the question Hardy stages with the help of his thrush. Does the thrush know something Hardy doesn't know, or is he only a beautiful little featherhead? There is not an answer to it, and thus there is not an answer as to whether it is Hardy who holds space for the thrush, or the thrush who holds space for him.

Mary Ruefle, disclaiming the possibility of knowing or saying anything about poetry in the introduction to a book of lectures about poetry, thinks of a thrush. "I do not think I really have anything to say about poetry other than remarking that it is a wandering little drift of unidentified sound," she comments.[6] To follow this sound, to try to know too much about it, is like following a thrush's song into the woods—you are unlikely to find him. "Fret not after knowledge, I have none," Ruefle's thrush says. "Perhaps we can use our knowledge to preserve a bit of space where his lack of knowledge can survive," she suggests.[7] Thus to have poetry, a person would hold poetry: leave it some room for its play of not mattering, through our not-knowing, as Milner left room for Simon's play. A poem says, "Why are you a fool?" I say, "Why am I a fool?" Or I say to the poem, why do you not matter? And it says to me, *why don't I matter?* The poem lets me call it foolish, if that is what I need. It's as hard to tell who plays the fool for whom as it is when we are in love.

how to come back to life

By this place full of fear,
By immense Chaos and the silence of this vast realm,
Reweave, I beg you, Eurydice's hurried fates.
We are all owed to you, and after a brief delay
Sooner or later we all rush down to this place.
This is our destination, our last home, and you
Hold the longest reign over the human race.
She too, after she has lived a normal span of years,
Will be yours by right. We are asking for a loan.

Ovid, *Metamorphoses*

They say that Orpheus turned back. The devil is in this detail. Eurydice has died by a snakebite. Orpheus, her grieving husband, harrows hell for her. All of us are owed to you, he says to Hades, but let her return for now. He pleads so movingly for Eurydice's life—"we are asking for a loan," he says, in Stanley Lombardo's translation of Ovid's *Metaphorphoses*— that Hades agrees. She can follow him over the rim of the world.[1] But there is one condition: her husband must keep his eyes facing upward, outward, until the two of them are through the gates. Orpheus, knowing this, turns back. Is Eurydice really following? Maybe she liked her taste of hell a bit more than she let on. Let's just check, he says, killing her. Ovid tells us she fades away without complaint. "What could she complain of except she was loved?"[2] What indeed? How about this senseless dashing of her chances, for starters? Why must the men always check? Othello strangles Desdemona, then cries about it. Lear stamps his foot for testimony from Cordelia. The men have to check. The women die.

Meanwhile, as Orpheus fretted, Eurydice was only confronting the fundamental human question: namely, shall I live at all? Orpheus turned back, but who cares about that? My question is, did Eurydice?

Let's say it was Eurydice alone who had to walk, straight as an arrow, out into the upper world. Let's say it was the middle of the road of her life, and she had to decide, shall I keep living? Let's say she was in her thirties, like Chris Kraus in *I Love Dick*. "She stands on the cliff of her life," Eileen Myles writes of Chris. The cliff is "approximately the same one, Jack Kerouac warned Neal Cassidy to not go over 'for nothing.' Which for those guys (fifties, alkies) was 30. For Chris it's 39. A female expiration date. And why? Chris' powerful account makes me wonder if all those bible stories that warn women not to turn around are just 'cause she might see something. Like her life."[3]

It's not that after some particular birthday, women in fact "expire," or go off; it's merely that some tiresome people think so, and that being invisible to such people confers a certain freedom. It's distracting to be wanted for dumb reasons—to be wanted *as* dumb—and to have to keep calculating whether you'll try to use that desire to your advantage or not. Myles is saying, think what happens when a gust of wind blows these admirers away, as though they were only so many gnats, and a woman can clear her head. This kind of "going over" is in some ways the opposite of what it meant to "go over" for Kerouac and Cassidy—although middle age is at issue in both cases. If the world was the men's oyster till they were thirty, thirty-nine is when Chris gets to stop being the oyster to men. If there is misery in no longer being desirable, there is liberty too. Now she can begin to think about what making the most of things would mean. The question life presents is no longer, am I wanted? but rather, do I want it? Life, that is.

Life is on Eurydice's hands, and she has to decide whether to walk up out of the underworld with it. So does Eurydice turn back? If she feels death's attractions, she is in good company. All over mythology we find people who have been told when they will die or what will kill them. It is supposed to be a curse. But this curse is also a wish. Without being in any way suicidal, a person can stand on a bridge and feel it would be, somehow, simpler to jump. A person can hold a knife and have the fleeting thought that since a knife must be plunged into one's gut sooner or later, literally or figuratively, it might as well be now. Edgar Allan Poe named the demon that prompts these thoughts "the Imp of the Perverse," in his 1845 tale of that title. Poe explained that a destructive impulse within us counters our every "desire to be well."[4] "Perversion" in a psychoanalytic sense, Adam Phillips suggests, is when we aim to still our desires by knowing what they are in advance. "To know beforehand is to assume that otherness, whether it be a person, a medium, an environment, is redundant; that it has nothing to offer us, that it brings nothing—or just rage and disappointment—to the occasion."[5] To think, let's just end it now, is to think that there is nothing worth having in the dilating uncertainty that stands between me and my eventual death.

It is not only in death itself that we encounter the temptation to prescind from life. "Eurydice recalls that death can claim us at any moment, in any of its forms," writes Dufourmantelle, "from renunciation to sacrifice, from anesthesia to dereliction."[6] What it means for death to claim us is that the sterile round of our routines claims us. We no longer see the point or the possibility of a pleasant surprise. We think, it would be better to have things *settled*. Death claims us in the passion some of us have for disposing of our lives, equally in the taking of excessive risks and in the settling of marriages. And those two things are not even incompatible: one can "sow one's wild oats" in the name of settling down. Beneath the placid surface presented by the well behaved is a panicked hunger to be tracked into a life of someone else's devising. Put me, I beg you, in a rut.

When we are perverse, we murder time. Hopeless that time will bring us anything good, we seek to fill it, to warp it, to make what we have left of it go away. Poe's Imp of the Perverse was also the patron saint of the cocktail party bore and the procrastinator. We are perverse, according to Poe, when we hold the listener past their endurance, when we who are "usually curt, precise, and clear" become seized with the thought, then the desire, of *delay*: we circumlocute, we hold, we fix the listener with our glittering eye. Or, genuinely wanting to turn to the task that is before us, we nonetheless hesitate.[7] Life can become oppressive, with its demand that we keep paddling and breathing without panicking. The Imp of the Perverse seems to show us a way out: by boring others or putting off work, he promises, we can take the minutes of our lives out of our hands. Phillips relays a story, passed down from Masud Kahn, of how Winnicott once spoke to an audience of Anglican priests. One of the priests asked how they would know that pastoral care was no longer enough and that the parishioner ought to be referred to a psychiatrist. Winnicott said, refer them if they bore you: "If a person comes and talks to you . . . and, listening to him, you feel he is boring you, then he is sick and needs psychiatric treatment. But if he sustains your interest, no matter how grave his distress or conflict, then you can help him all right."[8] Counterintuitively, it is not turmoil but placidity that betokens serious illness: the placidity of a flatline.

The self-sacrificing suicide and the deadening fulfillment of duty have in common their avoidance of the risk in the middle: "the risk of 'not yet dying,'" as Dufourmantelle puts it, this "gamble that we will always lose in the end, but only after traversing life with more or less plenitude, joy, and most of all, intensity."[9] In Poe's story, the final act of perversion is, in effect, to ask to be put to death, because not yet dying is something the narrator can no longer tolerate. Having committed an undetectable crime, the narrator of "The Imp of the Perverse" confesses it for no reason other than to master time once and for all. He speaks knowing he will be hanged in the morning. The crime is beside the point. The point is to end the uncertainty of his days. He cannot find the capacity to live a life to which no definite term has been set—one to whose occasion otherness might bring something other than rage and disappointment. It seems strange to say that the person who sets a term to his life has done so because he "know[s] exactly what [he] desire[s]."[10] But nonetheless there is a truth to it. He has prevented there from being anything that he could want, of which he hasn't already conceived.

In a case recounted by Dufourmantelle, the patient "Eurydice" has contrived to set a definite term to her life—not by courting her execution but by an inward certainty that she will not live past thirty. The thirties, to recall, are the age of "going over" for Myles and Kerouac too. Eurydice has always imagined death as an "appointment":

> It would be an appointment no more important than the dentist, an oil change, buying a pack of cigarettes. That morning, she knew, would be just a little more definitive than other mornings. And it wouldn't come from her. Certainly not! She was a stranger to any thought of killing herself, or even praying that chance would do it for her. She simply observed that she had a slight advantage over other people: knowing when the grim reaper would come to collect her.[11]

That death is an "appointment" tells us that this rendezvous is not about self-destruction, exactly, but about "definitiveness." Eurydice has felt she has an "advantage" in that her life is bounded more exactly than other people's. Knowing when death will come makes her life a well-appointed room, with sharp boundaries, rather than a vast and unmanageable space. But certainty also makes her life something less than a life. What takes her to psychoanalysis is the sudden appearance of a countervailing wish: perhaps she does, after all, want to live. This desire announces itself first as a fear of dying, a novel sensation for her. She has one session with an analyst, who says—with "stupidity," with "gentleness"—"Perhaps you want to live, a little bit more?"[12] Could she wish, really, for something so foolish?

She returns for another appointment, but the analyst is not there. It turns out that he has suddenly died, almost as if his death were a clinical intervention. Therapeutic actions in Dufourmantelle's cases have a folkloric tendency to take place partly beyond the consulting room, in the realm of life itself. Sometimes the analyst seems to live out, by sympathetic magic, an experience the patient needs to offload. The language game through which psychoanalysis helps, if it does, depends on viewing the patient's life as a kind of poetic making. The patient's acts and habits, their phobias and wishes, are to be listened to as if they were a way of speaking. In Dufourmantelle's depictions of the analytic scene, the analyst is not exempt, either, from this poetics of life.

Here, then, the analyst's death is an act of making. But it is not that he renounces his life in Eurydice's favor or that death takes him instead of her. "In the street, she knew that death had come to pass, that it took someone else. In her place? No, not even. It was just that she would no longer be there at the appointed time."[13] If the analyst's death has the function of signaling her release, it does so through a dream logic. The therapist dies; she lives. He does not keep their appointment for therapy; she does. Now she does not have to come again. Recombined, these elements yield: she kept her appointment with death. Death didn't show. Death *stood her up*—on her own feet, as if for the first time. She will walk up out of the underworld. She will not die yet.

At the end of Federico Fellini's *Le Notti di Cabiria* (1956), the actress Giulieta Masina stands up, turns away from her death, and walks back through the dusk to the upper world.[14] Masina plays Cabiria, an indomitably cheerful prostitute who has carefully saved over years to leave her profession and buy a house. She is in love; she thinks it's mutual; they marry. But it turns out he has planned all along to kill her and steal her life's savings. Soon after their wedding, he takes her to the edge of a cliff to see the sunset, then tries to push her off. She sees what he means to do just in time and saves herself.

But now, having snatched back her life, does she really want it? Not at first! She collapses in despair at her husband's feet, crying out again and again, "kill me! kill me! I don't want to live any longer!" He runs away, leaving the problem of life on her hands. The screen flickers to black, as if Cabiria has fainted. We see her again in the twilight. The sunset is over. She stands herself up. Her wedding suit is dusted with debris; a teardrop of mascara stands in the corner of her left eye. There is nothing for it but to walk uphill before darkness definitively falls—to walk out of Hades, following, albeit hours after, in the footsteps of her worthless Orpheus. The question that Fellini and Masina pose—they were creative partners, and married—is not whether he will look back. It's whether she will.

"Hell, you see," writes Dufourmantelle, "is an exact replica of the living world where you and I live. A surface projected into a cardboard eternity, where eras are superimposed on one another, from reflection to reflection."[15] But what is different in the living world is our consent not to know already everything there is to know. Not to model the desertions of the flim-flam man onto every young affair. Not to look behind, but to wonder what is up around the corner.

As Cabiria reaches the road, a little festival of spring suddenly weaves itself around her. For no reason that realism can furnish, dancers, an accordion player, and a couple on a moped populate the road. These happy fools try to include her. They are singing, dancing, covered in flowers. They look about twenty; she looks thirty-nine. She knows better; they do not. It is as if the dancers say to her, are you a fool? They are the fools. But she tucks the burden under her arm and says yes, I am a fool. She cheers up, though the tear-shaped smudge of mascara is still visible in her left eye. She gives a glance of puckish acknowledgment to each of the dancers, then to the camera, and to we fools beyond it too.

how to stay

An *ignis fatuus* is a swamp light, a wisp of phosphorescent gas that misguides travelers at night. They think it is the light of a human habitation. They head toward it. All they find is more wilderness. Eighteenth-century seduction fiction, warning women against sex out of wedlock, cautions them against these false lights. "Let not the magic arts of that worthless Sanford lead you, like an *ignis fatuus* from the path of rectitude and virtue!" a prudent friend warns an erring heroine about her seducer in Hannah Webster Foster's *The Coquette*.[1] But Emily Dickinson took a more sardonic view. "Better an ignis fatuus / Than no illume at all," she wrote.[2] She laments the loss of a secure belief in God in this poem. Better to believe in God and risk being wrong than to believe in nothing and find yourself rudderless. Some might think the point holds more generally. Better to believe in something—God, Love, Truth—than to fall into despair.

Is it better? Maybe it would be if those were the only two options. But those are not the only two options. There is also the possibility of being willing to wander, to fall into and out of patterns and phases, to riff. There is the possibility of following an ignis fatuus for a little while without having an inflated sense of the promise it holds out of rescue. There are patterns that can sustain you, even though they do not last forever, even though they do not mark up the world as known once and for all—even though they are not, strictly speaking, true.

The August when my sons were two, we visited our friends the painters, David and Jennifer, at their house in western Pennsylvania. Our friends Kurt and Tim and Eric were there as well. For many years, this group has returned in summer. Jennifer wonders whether the newts will also appear again in the streams each spring, whether the usual birds will nest, or whether they will have gone down with the planet's sinking ship. So far, like our friends, they return.

On the first night I was on childcare duty. I got stoned, and I thought it would be all right to go play drums in the barn late at night, while the children slept alone in a house far down the hill. John played guitar, David bass, Tim keyboards. I set a timer on my watch, and every twenty minutes I stumbled down the hill, the light on my phone an ignis fatuus, to check for sound. My sons soundly slept. Then I would return to the barn and play.

What I liked was to hit the kick and the snare on the one and the three. Then it would occasionally seem as if it might be possible to have more, as if I could put in a small riff. But it was impossible to decide where the small riff should land, to coordinate thinking, hearing, raising my hand. All of these gestures had to happen prior to the beat, in a simultaneousness of volition and action, but the impulse I had to do them did not begin until the beat had already started to fall. I gave it up, and I was more than contented to give it up. I stuck to the one and the three. Even within this sameness, there was change.

Keeping a rhythm means forgetting the rhythm, not stopping to think either before or behind, watching the other players. To hit the drum, to check the beat against the better players in the warm light of the barn, with the riding lawnmower over past the beams—light glinting on the powder-blue drums—this was enough. I could look to John to see if it was all right because I knew he knew. I could see from his face that I was happy.

In the morning I looked at him again, wide-eyed at the thought of the risk I had taken. What had I been thinking? What if our children had woken in the pitch dark? What if they had gotten to the door? What about the pond below the house? But none of these things had happened. He shrugged, which is to say, he shouldered with me the burden of my decision; he concealed from me that any burden had been lifted.

It was not until the next year's visit that my son, in full view of four sober adults, slipped into the pond, and John crashed in to scoop him up. We shrugged it off. We all told each other *it's OK*; we moved on briskly for the child's sake and did not speak of it. But my son does speak of it. *Story bout I fell into the pond*, he demands. I tell the story. He says he doesn't want to fall into a pond again. I tell him his father and I will always be near if he is near water, and we will scoop him up. This is not true. But I'll be his fool.

Acknowledgments

"How to Have a One-Night Stand" appeared at *Berfrois*, "How to Come Back to Life" appeared in the *Yale Review*, summer 2021 issue, and earlier versions or parts of the following chapters appeared at *3 Quarks Daily*: "How to Hold It Together," "How to Turn the Corner," "How to Listen," "How to Hope," and "How to Come Back to Life." I thank the editors for permission to reprint.

Alan Thomas, Randolph Petilos, Levi Stahl, and the rest of the talented staff at the University of Chicago Press made this book a thing in the world. I am grateful to Jess Swoboda for meticulous fact-checking and to Lisa Wehrle for tactful copyediting.

Matt Bevis, Todd Carmody, Pete Coviello, Jonathan Elmer, Erica Fretwell, Nick Gaskill, Erica McAlpine, John Parker, Lindsay Reckson, Alan Thomas, and Johanna Winant read all or most of this book in manuscript. They reassured and criticized, praised and questioned. I deeply appreciate all these offices of friendship.

notes

HOW TO CATCH A MINNOW

1. Revelation 3.2 (NRSV).
2. Revelation 2.4 (NRSV).
3. Elizabeth Hardwick, *Sleepless Nights* (New York: New York Review Books, 2001), 5.
4. Herman Melville, *Moby-Dick; or, The Whale* (Evanston, IL: Northwestern University Press, 1988), 169.
5. Tony J. Pitcher and Julia K. Parrish, "Functions of Shoaling Behaviour in Teleosts," in *Behaviour of Teleost Fishes*, 2nd ed., ed. Tony J. Pitcher (London: Chapman & Hall, 1993), 380.
6. Anne Dufourmantelle, *In Praise of Risk*, trans. Steven Miller (New York: Fordham University Press, 2019), 120–21.

HOW TO SWIM

1. Ralph Waldo Emerson, "Experience," in *Essays: First and Second Series*, ed. Joel Porte (New York: Library of America, 1990), 241.
2. Emily Dickinson, 407 ["One need not be a chamber to be haunted"], in *The Poems of Emily Dickinson*, Variorum ed., ed. R. W. Franklin (Cambridge, MA: Belknap Press of Harvard University Press, 1998), 1:431.

3. Melville, *Moby-Dick*, 376.

4. Revelation 13.1 (NRSV).

5. Walcott quoted in Dionne Brand, *A Map to the Door of No Return: Notes to Belonging* (Toronto: Vintage Canada, 2011), 12.

6. Brand, *Map to the Door of No Return*, 11–12.

7. Brand, *Map to the Door of No Return*, 185.

8. Brand, *Map to the Door of No Return*, 185.

9. Émile Durkheim, *The Elementary Forms of Religious Life*, trans. Karen E. Fields (New York: Free Press, 1995), 9–17.

10. Edward Sapir, "The Unconscious Patterning of Behavior in Society," in *The Collected Works of Edward Sapir*, ed. Regna Darnell and Judith T. Irvine (Berlin: Mouton de Gruyter, 1999), 3:156–72.

11. Sapir, "Unconscious Patterning of Behavior," 159.

12. Sapir, "Unconscious Patterning of Behavior," 161.

13. Sapir, "Unconscious Patterning of Behavior," 158.

14. Melville, *Moby-Dick*, 388.

HOW TO HOLD IT TOGETHER

1. Frederick Douglass, "What to the Slave Is the Fourth of July? Extract from an Oration, at Rochester, July 5, 1852," in *My Bondage and My Freedom* (New York: Penguin, 2003), 344.

2. Sigmund Freud, "Fetishism," in *The Complete Psychological Works of Sigmund Freud*, vol. 21, trans. James Strachey (London: Hogarth and the Institute of Psychoanalysis, 1957), 147–57.

3. Pamela Klassen, *The Story of Radio Mind* (Chicago: University of Chicago Press, 2018), 10.

HOW TO GIVE BIRTH

1. Mary Ruefle, *Madness, Rack, and Honey: Collected Lectures* (Seattle: Wave Books, 2012), 261.

2. Stephen Wilson, *The Magical Universe: Everyday Ritual and Magic in Pre-Modern Europe* (New York: Hambledon and London, 2000), 123–24.

3. William Shakespeare, Sonnet 116, in *Shakespeare's Sonnets*, ed. Stephen Booth (New Haven, CT: Yale University Press, 1977), 100.

4. Shakespeare, Sonnet 30, in Booth, *Shakespeare's Sonnets*, 28.

HOW TO MILK

1. D. W. Winnicott, "Transitional Objects and Transitional Phenomena: A Study of the First Not-Me Possession," *International Journal of Psychoanalysis* 34 (1953): 93.

2. Adam Phillips, *On Kissing, Tickling, and Being Bored* (Cambridge, MA: Harvard University Press, 1993), 34.

3. Phillips, *On Kissing, Tickling, and Being Bored*, 34.

4. Wilson, *Magical Universe*, 435.

HOW TO STEP OVER A SNAKE

1. Wallace Stevens, "Anecdote of the Jar," in *The Collected Poems of Wallace Stevens* (New York: Alfred A. Knopf, 1968), 76.

2. Hardwick, *Sleepless Nights*, 105.

3. Hardwick, *Sleepless Nights*, 9.

4. Hardwick, *Sleepless Nights*, 9.

5. Hardwick, *Sleepless Nights*, 38.

6. Stevens, "The Planet on the Table," in *Collected Poems*, 532.

7. Percy Bysshe Shelley, *The Poetical Works of Shelley*, ed. Newell F. Ford (Boston: Hougton Mifflin, 1974), 366.

8. John Keats, ["This living hand, now warm and capable"], in *Keats: Poetical Works*, ed. H. W. Garrod (Oxford: Oxford University Press, 1970), 438.

9. Hardwick, *Sleepless Nights*, 76.

HOW TO HERD

1. Melville, *Moby-Dick*, 280–81.
2. *Oxford English Dictionary Online*, 3rd ed. (2014), s.v. "ornery," "cussed."
3. Brian Blanchfield, *Proxies: Essays Near Knowing* (New York: Nightboat Books, 2017), 23.
4. Iona Opie, ed., *My Very First Mother Goose*, illus. Rosemary Wells (Somerville, MA: Candlewick Press, 1996), 62–63.

HOW TO RIFF

1. *Oxford English Dictionary Online*, s.v. "riff," n.5.
2. Melville, *Moby-Dick*, 188.
3. Melville, *Moby-Dick*, 189.
4. Melville, *Moby-Dick*, 193.
5. Melville, *Moby-Dick*, 195.
6. Melville, *Moby-Dick*, 195.
7. Steve Reich, "Piano Phase for 2 Pianos or 2 Marimbas" (1967; New York: Universal Edition, 1980), [3].
8. Meredith L. McGill, "What Is a Ballad? Reading for Genre, Format, and Medium," *Nineteenth-Century Literature* 71, no. 2 (2016): 163–64.
9. Aretha Franklin, "Amazing Grace," recorded January 13, 1972, at New Temple Missionary Baptist Church, Los Angeles, CA, *Amazing Grace* (Atlantic Records, double LP, 1972; remastered double compact disc, 1999).

HOW TO TURN THE CORNER

1. Stephen Holden, "Blossom Dearie, Cult Chanteuse, Dies at 84," *New York Times*, February 8, 2009.
2. Blossom Dearie, "I Walk a Little Faster," music by Cy Coleman and lyrics by Carolyn Leigh, on *Give Him the Ooh-La-La* (Verve, LP 1978).

3. Hardwick, *Sleepless Nights*, 37.

4. Hardwick, *Sleepless Nights*, 51.

5. James Baldwin, *The Fire Next Time*, in *Collected Essays* (New York: Library of America, 1998), 8.

6. Baldwin, *Collected Essays*, 292.

7. David Lynch, *Blue Velvet* (1986; Burbank, CA: Warner Home Video, 1991).

8. Baldwin, *Collected Essays*, 311.

9. Les Blue Stars, *Lullaby of Birdland and Other Famous Hits* (Mercury, LP 1956); Les Blue Stars, *Octuor* (Barclay, 10-inch, [1954–55]); Les Blue Stars, *Lullaby of Birdland* (Mercury, 7-inch, 1955). See also Holden, "Blossom Dearie."

10. Les Blue Stars, *Lullaby of Birdland* (Mercury, 7-inch, 1955).

HOW TO HAVE A ONE-NIGHT STAND

1. Anna Burns, *Milkman* (Minneapolis: Graywolf, 2018), 133.

2. Hardwick, *Sleepless Nights*, 55.

3. Edgar Allan Poe, *Poetry and Tales* (New York: Library of America, 1984), 398.

4. Hardwick, *Sleepless Nights*, 57.

5. Poe, *Poetry and Tales*, 401.

6. Charles Baudelaire, *The Painter of Modern Life and Other Essays*, trans. and ed. Jonathan Mayne (New York: Phaidon Press, 1994), 7.

HOW TO LISTEN

1. Dufourmantelle, *In Praise of Risk*, 20.

2. Dufourmantelle, *In Praise of Risk*, 20.

3. Muriel Spark, *The Prime of Miss Jean Brodie, The Girls of*

Slender Means, The Driver's Seat, The Only Problem (New York: Everyman, 2004), 29.

4. Phillips, *On Kissing, Tickling, and Being Bored*, 63.
5. George Oppen, "Technologies," in *New Collected Poems*, ed. Michael Davidson, preface by Eliot Weinberger (New York: New Directions, 2002), 93.

HOW TO HAVE A BREAKTHROUGH

1. Revelation 1.19 (NRSV).
2. Wilson, *Magical Universe*, 98.
3. Blanchfield, *Proxies*, 155.
4. Mona Van Duyn, "The Stream," in *Letters from a Father and Other Poems* (New York: Atheneum, 1982), 16–17.

HOW TO LOVE

1. Poe, *Poetry and Tales*, 555.
2. Emerson, "Experience," 243.
3. Emerson, "Experience," 242.
4. Emerson, "Experience," 257.
5. Emerson, "Experience," 252–54, 258.
6. Emerson, "Experience," 260.

HOW TO ELUDE YOUR CAPTORS

1. Ruefle, *Madness, Rack, and Honey*, 103.
2. Stanley Cavell, *The Claim of Reason: Wittgenstein, Skepticism, Morality, and Tragedy* (New York: Oxford University Press, 1979), 33.
3. Italo Calvino, *Six Memos for the Next Millennium*, trans. Geoffrey Brock (Boston: Mariner Books, 2016), 14.
4. Calvino, *Six Memos*, 8.
5. Calvino, *Six Memos*, 6.

6. Emily Dickinson, 359 ["A Bird, came down the Walk"], in *Poems of Emily Dickinson*, 1:384–85.

HOW TO HOPE

1. Thomas Hardy, "The Darkling Thrush," in *Collected Poems of Thomas Hardy* (London: Macmillan, 1919), 137. The poem was first published as "By the Century's Deathbed," in *The Graphic*, December 29, 1900.
2. Hardy, *Collected Poems*, 137.
3. Emerson, "Experience," 252.
4. David Russell, *Tact: Aesthetic Liberalism and the Essay Form in Nineteenth-Century Britain* (Princeton, NJ: Princeton University Press, 2018), 142–50.
5. Milner, quoted in Russell, *Tact*, 149–50.
6. Ruefle, *Madness, Rack, and Honey*, viii.
7. Ruefle, *Madness, Rack, and Honey*, viii.

HOW TO COME BACK TO LIFE

1. Ovid, *Metamorphoses*, trans. Stanley Lombardo (Indianapolis: Hackett, 2010), 10:38.
2. Ovid, *Metamorphoses*, 10:64.
3. Eileen Myles, foreword to *I Love Dick*, by Chris Kraus (Los Angeles: Semiotext(e), 1998), 14.
4. Poe, *Poetry and Tales*, 828.
5. Phillips, *On Kissing, Tickling, and Being Bored*, 63.
6. Dufourmantelle, *In Praise of Risk*, 180.
7. Poe, *Poetry and Tales*, 828.
8. Adam Phillips, *Winnicott* (Cambridge, MA: Harvard University Press, 1988), 25.
9. Dufourmantelle, *In Praise of Risk*, 180.
10. Phillips, *On Kissing, Tickling, and Being Bored*, 63.
11. Dufourmantelle, *In Praise of Risk*, 4.

12. Dufourmantelle, *In Praise of Risk*, 5.
13. Dufourmantelle, *In Praise of Risk*, 6.
14. Federico Fellini, *Le Notti di Cabiria* (1956; Irvington, NY: Criterion Collection, 1999).
15. Dufourmantelle, *In Praise of Risk*, 182.

HOW TO STAY
 1. Hannah Webster Foster, *The Coquette*, ed. Cathy N. Davidson (New York: Oxford University Press, 1986), 57.
 2. Emily Dickinson, 1581 ["Those dying then"], in *Poems of Emily Dickinson*, 3:1386.